sharing with travellers a wealth of
experience and a passion for travel.

**Rely on Thomas Cook as your
travelling companion on your next trip
and benefit from our unique heritage.**

Thomas Cook **pocket** guides

VENICE

Written by Anwer Bati, updated by Jo-Ann Titmarsh

Published by Thomas Cook Publishing
A division of Thomas Cook Tour Operations Limited
Company registration no. 3772199 England
The Thomas Cook Business Park, Unit 9, Coningsby Road,
Peterborough PE3 8SB, United Kingdom
Email: books@thomascook.com, Tel: +44 (0) 1733 416477
www.thomascookpublishing.com

Produced by Cambridge Publishing Management Limited
Burr Elm Court, Main Street, Caldecote CB23 7NU
www.cambridgepm.co.uk

ISBN: 978-1-84848-414-6

© 2006, 2008 Thomas Cook Publishing
This third edition © 2011 Thomas Cook Publishing
Text © Thomas Cook Publishing
Maps © Thomas Cook Publishing/PCGraphics (UK) Limited
Transport map © Communicarta Limited

Series Editor: Karen Beaulah
Production/DTP: Steven Collins

Printed and bound in Spain by GraphyCems

Cover photography © Cezare White

CONTENTS

SYMBOLS KEY

The following symbols are used throughout this book:

ⓐ address ☎ telephone ✆ fax Ⓦ website address ⓔ email
🕐 opening times Ⓝ public transport connections ❶ important

The following symbols are used on the maps:

𝒊 information office	▢ point of interest
✈ airport	⊟ railway station
✚ hospital	Ⓥ vaporetto
🛡 police station	✝ cathedral
🚌 bus station	— railway
❶ numbers denote featured cafés & restaurants	

Hotels and restaurants are graded by approximate price as follows:
£ budget price **££** mid-range price **£££** expensive

▶ *The cupolas of St Mark's Basilica*

INTRODUCING
Venice

Introduction

The Italian city of Venezia, or Venice, right at the tip of the Adriatic Sea, has always been a source of inspiration for artists, writers and romantics. Its spectacular watery landscape may be familiar the world over, but close up its beauty still has the power to beguile you. And despite its diminutive size, there is so much to see – something alluring or intriguing around virtually every corner.

Perhaps the city is all the more romantic for its fragility. *La Serenissima*, or 'The Most Serene', as it was once known, is built on a series of small, swampy islands connected by around 400 footbridges. With the islands gradually sinking on their unstable foundations, rising sea levels threaten to flood the area and destroy some of the world's most precious works of art and architecture. Now is a historic time to visit this historic city.

But tourism is not a new phenomenon in Venice. Touring aristocrats and wealthy visitors have always flocked here to enjoy the city's one-time great wealth, influence and cultural activity. As a naval power and a major port and trading hub in the 13th–15th centuries, affluent local traders and well-heeled philanthropists vied with each other to commission bigger, grander, more ornate buildings and works of art, and culture lovers scrambled to see the results. Fashionable gentlemen and ladies came for the riotous carnival celebrations, banned by successive governments but still alive today.

Now it is mostly tourism that keeps the city alive, protects the historic monuments and stimulates the economy. Travelling around Venice by boat, admiring some of the world's most magnificent art and architecture and taking part in centuries-old festivals and traditions are unique experiences. Prices can be fairly high and the weather can be dull at times, but visitors keep flocking. If you visit too, you will understand why.

🔺 *A rainbow over Riva degli Schiavoni*

When to go

Venice welcomes tourists at any time of the year but is particularly busy between Easter and October. This long high season corresponds with high prices, packed accommodation and long queues. The city also fills up over Christmas and New Year and during its carnival in February. The best time to visit is early spring or late autumn to avoid the crowds and high prices, or in November or January if you want a quiet stay and don't mind the cold, damp weather.

SEASONS & CLIMATE

Venice tends to be hot and humid in summer, with the odd thunderstorm. Spring and autumn are mild but wet and the easterly wind can make for chilly evenings. Venice is cold, foggy and damp in winter, which can be romantic if you are well protected and wrapped up warm. High tides (*acqua alta*) and winds in winter can sometimes lead to flooding in the city.

ANNUAL EVENTS

The most important cultural events in Venice, apart from Carnival, are the alternate Art and Architecture Biennale festivals held throughout the summer and the International Film Festival in September. Some of the most attractive celebrations to attend, however, are the smaller, more traditional events such as the gondola race on the feast day of St Mark or the 1,000-year-old ceremony of La Sensa.

January

Regata delle Befane The first of many rowing regattas during the year, held on Epiphany (6 Jan). The race takes place along the

Grand Canal, with usually one or two male competitors per boat dressed as the good witch Befana. According to local legend, Befana visits the city the night before Epiphany and delivers sweets and gifts to good children.

February
Carnevale (Carnival, see page 12) A colourful riot of processions, parties and street theatre in the ten days leading up to Lent.

April
Festa di San Marco The feast day of Venice's patron saint St Mark, 25 April, is celebrated by a gondola race from the island of Sant'Elena to the Punta della Dogana on the Grand Canal.

May–July
La Sensa A thousand-year-old ceremony off the Lido, in which the mayor of Venice throws a gold ring into the sea to symbolise Venice's 'marriage' to the waters. The event takes place on the Sunday after Ascension Day.

Vogalonga Hundreds of boats take part in a race open to anyone in a rowing vessel – however outlandish – including visitors. The race is held on a Sunday in May or early June and starts at 08.30 from St Mark's Square, heralded by a cannon shot. It takes place along a very scenic, winding 30-km (18½-mile) course. ❶ 041 521 0544 ⓦ www.vogalonga.it

Biennale d'Arte Contemporanea Venice's Biennial Contemporary Arts Festival, founded in 1895, takes place on odd-numbered years and sees both official and unofficial exhibitions and events at various locations including the Giardini park and the Arsenale. ❶ 041 521 8711 ⓦ www.labiennale.org ❶ 10.00–18.00 Tues–Sun,

(mid-June–end Oct), closed Mon. Next arts festivals 2011, 2013
❶ Admission charge to official exhibitions

Biennale d'Architettura (Biennial Architecture Festival) Takes
place on even-numbered years. Details as for the Biennale d'Arte.
Next architecture festivals 2012, 2014.

Venezia Suona One-day rock, folk and jazz festival, usually held on
a Sunday in late June. ❶ 041 275 0049 Ⓦ www.veneziasuona.it

Festa del Redentore One of Venice's oldest and most important
festivals celebrating the end of the plague of 1576. A pontoon
bridge is constructed across the Giudecca Canal to the church
of Il Redentore (see page 124) on the third weekend in July. Boats and
picnickers gather to celebrate and there is a spectacular firework
display in the evening.

August & September

Mostra Internazionale D'Arte Cinematografica (Venice International
Film Festival, see page 122) One of the world's most important
film festivals, based on the Lido.

Circuito Off Venice International Short Film Festival Quieter film
festival held over one week in early September on the tiny island
of San Servolo. Many films are in English. ➐ Giudecca 212
❶ 041 244 6979 ❶ 041 244 6930 Ⓦ www.circuitooff.com

Regata Storica Colourful parade of decorated boats on the first
Sunday in September, followed by rowing races with participants
wearing historical costumes.

October

Venice Marathon Held between Stra, east of Padua, and the Riva
dei Sette Martiri on the last Sunday in October. ❶ 041 532 1871
Ⓦ www.venicemarathon.it

November
Festa della Salute Festival celebrating the end of the plague of 1630.
A bridge of boats is laid across the Grand Canal to the church of
Santa Maria della Salute on 21 November, a public holiday in Venice.

PUBLIC HOLIDAYS
Capodanno (New Year's Day) 1 Jan
La Befana (Epiphany) 6 Jan
Pasqua & Pasquetta (Easter Sunday & Monday) 24–5 Apr 2011,
8–9 Apr 2012, 31 Mar–1 Apr 2013
Festa della Liberazione/Festa di San Marco (Liberation Day) 25 Apr
Festa del Lavoro (Labour Day) 1 May
Festa della Repubblica (Anniversary of the Republic) 2 June
Festa di San Giovanni (Feast of St John the Baptist) 24 June
Ferragosto (Feast of the Assumption) 15 Aug
Ognissanti (All Saints' Day) 1 Nov
Festa della Salute (Venice only) 21 Nov
Festa dell'Immacolata (Feast of the Immaculate Conception) 8 Dec
Natale (Christmas) 25 Dec
Santo Stefano (Boxing Day) 26 Dec

Businesses, banks and post offices are closed on public
holidays and there is limited public transport on 1 May,
Christmas Day and New Year's Day. Shops and restaurants
tend to stay open on public holidays in Venice, unlike in
the rest of Italy.

Carnival

Venice's *carnevale* (carnival), first held in 1162, was the precursor to modern carnivals around the world. Although the name literally means 'farewell to meat', since it was held in the days running up to Lent, the event also signalled a farewell to ordinary social hierarchy and discipline. Masks disguised people's identity and class, leading to a slackening of social mores. Numerous laws were introduced to restrict the festivities, including an outright ban by Napoleon in 1797. Revived but then banned again in the 1930s by a fascist government, official carnival celebrations only restarted in 1979.

The carnival opens each year on the Sunday ten days before *martedì grasso* (Shrove Tuesday) with a grand procession and the Flight of the Dove – a spectacular event in which a trapeze-walking acrobat or an artificial dove flies from the Campanile to the Doge's Palace. Events centre around St Mark's Square with activities such as face-painting, ice-skating, street theatre and live music throughout the ten days. There are several exclusive parties including the legendary Ridotto ball at the **Monaco Hotel** (W www.hotelmonaco.it). Details of planned events throughout the carnival, which is run and partly sponsored by the city council, appear on the Internet around the end of January. Check W www.carnivalofvenice.com or W www.turismovenezia.it for details.

One major feature of Carnival is the fantastic range of elaborate masks available to buy, hire or simply admire – anything from *commedia dell'arte* characters to Disney (see page 24).

Hiring carnival costumes can cost anything from €80 to €600. Try **Nicolao Atelier** (a Cannaregio 2590, Fondamenta della Misericordia ① 041 520 7051 W www.nicolao.com) or **Atelier Pietro Longhi** (a San Polo 2608, Rio Terà Frari ① 041 714 478 W www.pietrolonghi.com).

⬥ *Carnival masks make beautiful but pricey souvenirs*

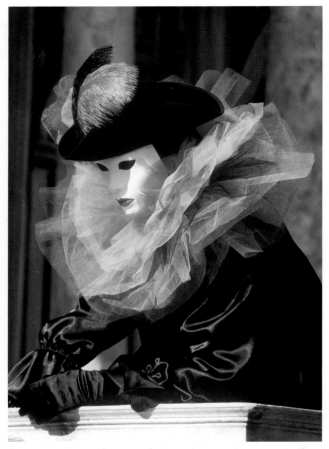

⬤ *Spectacular costumes compete for attention during Carnival*

CASANOVA

Giovanni Giacomo Casanova (1725–98) demonstrates perfectly the loose spirit of Carnival in 18th-century Venice with his well-known life of drinking, partying and whirlwind affairs.

The tall, dark Italian dandy originally studied clerical law in Venice but his short career in the Church was tainted by scandals and he quickly left to join the army. Unsuited to the austere military life, Casanova returned to the attractions of Venice where he saved the life of a rich nobleman – thus ensuring his own wealth and position in society. A practical joke involving a freshly buried corpse went wrong when the victim died of shock, and this combined with a rape allegation drove Casanova to leave the city.

Returning to his home town at the age of 30, he was soon arrested and imprisoned in the Doge's Palace (see page 66) for his interest in witchcraft. The only prisoner ever to escape from here, he travelled all round Europe leaving a trail of extraordinary scandals in his wake and eventually came back to Venice – only to be expelled once again for a vicious satire poking fun at the nobility. Perhaps the most extraordinary fact about this notoriously wild philanderer's life is that he died quietly as a librarian in what is now the Czech Republic.

❶ If you want to take part in the carnival, book well in advance and be prepared to pay high prices. The opening Sunday, Shrove Tuesday and the weekend are the most lively times but the city can be extremely crowded. Streets become bottlenecked and there is a real danger of small children getting lost or crushed in the crowds.

History

Venice was founded in the middle of the 5th century when the Lombards and other Germanic tribes invaded northern Italy. Fleeing Italians sought refuge on the islands of the Venetian lagoon and in 697 formed a republic ruled by an elected doge, or 'duke'. Technically still under Byzantine rule, the community gradually increased its independence and a grand palazzo was erected on the site of the present Doge's Palace (see page 66) in the early 9th century.

St Mark was allegedly adopted as the city's patron saint in 828 and the saint's symbol, a winged lion, became the city's emblem. St Mark's Basilica, one of the most popular and impressive buildings in Venice, was originally built as a shrine to his remains in the 9th century.

The Republic of Venice developed a superficially democratic system of government, with elected doges staying in power for life but constrained by councils. In reality, the city-state was controlled by an oligarchy of nobles and merchants.

It wasn't long before the hardy republic became a military and trading force to be reckoned with. Strong links with the Byzantine empire and a powerful navy allowed the city to defeat several rivals in the area, including Cyprus and Crete, and to take control of large portions of the mainland. Power brought arrogance and aggression abroad. Venetians were foremost in the sacking of Constantinople in 1204, returning to their city with huge amounts of booty.

The 15th century saw the city's zenith, when it was the acknowledged leading power in the eastern Mediterranean and the most substantial naval force in Christendom.

The 16th century brought economic and cultural prosperity but a decline in its military and naval empire. In 1797 Napoleon invaded and deposed the last doge, Ludovico Manin, giving control of the city to the Habsburg monarchy of Austria. Apart from a short period of French rule (1805–15), Venice remained part of Austria until joining Italy in 1866.

Although the port and industrial areas at Marghera and the office buildings at Mestre were developed in the early 20th century, with vastly improved rail and road links, Venice's main industry is now tourism.

SINKING CITY

Venice rests precariously on the unstable, swampy islands of a lagoon. It has been gradually sinking for years, but rising sea levels have recently increased the threat that the city will be inundated, possibly obliterated, by water.

Already when storm winds blow across the Adriatic Sea from the south, the waters pile up and *acqua alta* or 'high water' regularly floods the city. Wooden walkways are erected to help pedestrians get about but the salt water is damaging both the ancient buildings and their foundations. You can often see a line of green algae on the outside of buildings marking the frighteningly high water level.

In 2001 the Italian government set in motion an elaborate dam project in the form of 79 enormous hinged gates to close off the lagoon at high water. The plan is controversial, with many experts believing that frequent gate closings will turn the lagoon into an unhealthy pool of industrial waste and sewage. Venice was declared a World Heritage Site by UNESCO in 1987 but even this status may not be enough to save it from a watery end.

Lifestyle

Compared to the estimated 13 or 14 million tourists who visit the city each year, Venice's native population of just 65,000 is very much outnumbered. High prices and very little industry drive residents either into the hospitality business or into leaving Venice to seek work elsewhere. Very few Venetians now live in the centre.

It is fascinating to see the extent to which Venice's waterborne transport system affects the daily life of locals. With no cars to fill up on a weekly supermarket run, inhabitants tend to shop daily in local grocery stores and bakeries. Postmen, rubbish collectors, doctors and ambulances must all travel by water rather than by road. Even crossing the main 'street', the Grand Canal, can involve a short ride over the water on a *traghetto*.

GONDOLA TRIP

To re-enact a classic image of Venice, take a gondola trip around the canals. The boats take up to six people and singers can be arranged at an extra cost.

The best place to arrange a tour is at an official gondola stop, at the Valaresso, San Tomà and Ca d'Oro water bus stops; at the railway station and bus terminal; at Fondamenta Bacino Orseolo behind St Mark's Square; on Riva degli Schiavoni; in Campo San Moisè; and on the San Polo side of Rialto Bridge. Prices are fixed officially by the Gondola Board at €80 for 40 mins between 8am and 7pm, €100 for 50 mins between 7pm and 8am plus €50 for each additional 30 mins. There is no need to pay over the official rate. Most speak some English. See Ⓦ www.gondolieri.it

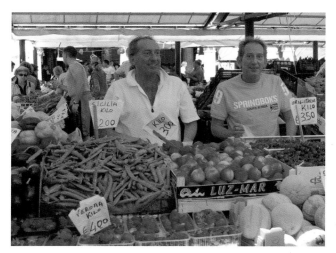

● *Venice's covered market on the Rialto – a taste of local life*

The tourist industry also has a great influence on Venetian lifestyle. The demand for handmade arts and crafts means that many locals have acquired considerable artistic skill, reviving traditional techniques of mask-making, glass-blowing and lacemaking. Many speak English. In contrast to other European countries, summer is the time when most Venetians work hardest, taking their holidays only when low tourist season arrives.

Inevitably for such a small and popular place, prices are high all year round and rocket in summer and over Christmas, New Year and during Carnival. Cut down on costs by doing as the locals do: use water buses not taxis; choose restaurants away from the centre; and drink your coffee standing at the bar rather than sitting at a table.

Culture

Travelling around the canals by water bus or taxi is the best way to get a flavour of Venice's impressive cultural history. Look out for the different architectural styles. Thirteenth-century Byzantine-influenced palazzos have characteristic simple rounded arches, contrasting with the elaborate pointed arches and tracery of Gothic 14th- and 15th-century buildings such as the **Ca' d'Oro** (see page 110) and the **Doge's Palace** (see page 66). Sandstone Renaissance structures with classical columns stand among the heavily ornamented Baroque buildings of the 17th century, such as **Ca' Pesaro** (see page 97). There is little modern architecture in Venice and most building work these days is for maintenance and renovation.

Venice's biggest boast in architecture is the hugely influential Andrea di Pietro della Gondola (1508–80). Nicknamed Palladio after the Greek goddess of wisdom Pallas Athene, his harmonious designs adhere strongly to classical Roman principles and the 'Palladian style' has become a recognised architectural style in itself. Many of his celebrated buildings and churches, scattered around Venice and the Veneto region, were given special status in 1994 as a UNESCO World Heritage Site known as the Palladian Villas of the Veneto.

Venice's many churches, each set in their own small square, or *campo*, are not only architecturally delightful in themselves but also boast works of art which would grace any major museum.

Venetian artists over the years have left a hoard of valuable paintings reflecting the wealth of their city and the sophistication and finery of some of its citizens. Paolo Veneziano and his contemporaries in the 14th century, influenced by Byzantine art, were the first painters to make a lasting mark on the art world but it was the brothers Giovanni and Gentile Bellini, in the following century, who became internationally famous for their vivid, colourful style. Many of their works can be found in the **Correr Museum** (see page 70).

The greatest Venetian masters from the 16th century onwards, including Titian, Veronese, Giorgione and Tintoretto, began to use oil rather than egg-based tempera paint. This allowed them to exploit more fully the subtle use of light, shade, atmosphere and texture. You can see some of their finest and best-known works in the **Accademia Gallery** (see page 85).

The 18th century saw the last great movement of Venetian art with painters such as Giambattista Tiepolo, and his son Giandomenico. Canaletto is probably the most famous 18th-century landscape painter ever. Many of his classic images of Venice are now in Britain, bought by aristocrats on the Grand Tour.

For modern art, it's best to visit during the **Biennale**, a major contemporary arts festival held every two years in summer and packed with fantastic exhibitions (see page 9). There are also some

🔺 *La Fenice opera house hosts opera, drama and ballet*

excellent collections of modern art at the **Guggenheim Museum** (see page 86), **Palazzo Grassi** (see page 67) and **Ca' Pesaro** (see page 97).

If you enjoy the performing arts and you speak Italian, it is worth seeing a play at the beautiful **Teatro Carlo Goldoni** (❸ San Marco 4650B, Calle Goldoni ❶ 041 240 2011 Ⓦ www.teatrostabileveneto.it Ⓝ Water bus to Rialto). There are also performances of opera, dance and ballet at the **La Fenice** opera house (see feature, page 64) and the **Teatro Malibran** (see page 118). Contemporary dance events are usually held at the **Teatro Fondamenta Nuove** (see page 118).

Concerts of classical music and opera are held around the city and are particularly pleasant when held in a church. There is the occasional live jazz session but strict noise-reduction laws mean concerts of rock and other contemporary music are rare. Book well in advance for major concerts, particularly during peak season.

COMBINED TICKETS

If you plan to visit several cultural attractions, it is well worth getting a combined ticket. You can browse the options at any tourist office and at the ACTV-Vela offices at Piazzale Roma and near St Mark's Square (❶ 041 2424 ❶ 08.00–20.00 daily).

The **Chorus Pass** allows you entrance to Venice's main churches and is available from any of the churches which charge for entry. See Ⓦ www.chorusvenezia.org

The **Venice Card**, which entitles you to free public transport, use of public toilets and entry to various sights and attractions, is another good option. See Ⓦ www.hellovenezia.com

❍ *Gondolas at a busy intersection*

MAKING THE MOST OF
Venice

Shopping

Venice's designer clothes shops are clustered around the Mercerie area near St Mark's Square, including some excellent leather shoe and accessory shops.

Skilled artisans selling their arts and crafts are mostly based around Campo Santo Stefano, Calle della Mandola and the Dorsoduro district. The art of making marbled paper was revived in the 1970s and you will see several styles of beautiful paper and other stationery on offer.

There are some good antiques shops clustered around Campo San Maurizio, near St Mark's Square. Look out for rich local fabrics, jewellery, metalwork and old prints.

LOCAL SPECIALITIES

Genuine local specialities from Venice can make fine gifts or souvenirs. Look out for beautiful lace, marbled paper, glass and carnival masks, produced by skilled local artisans. Glass is best bought on the island of **Murano** (see page 135), where you can see the glass objects being blown, and lace is particularly fine on **Burano** (see page 137). However, be wary of shops selling inferior, imported versions of these products. Be prepared to pay for quality.

The traditional art of mask-making was revived in 1979 and there are several shops making papier mâché masks. Two of the best are **Mondo Novo** (Dorsoduro 3063, Rio Terra Canal 041 528 7344 09.00–18.00 Mon–Sat, closed Sun Water bus to Ca' Rezzonico) and **Papier Mâché** (Castello 5175, Calle Lunga Santa Maria Formosa 041 522 9995 09.00–19.30 Mon–Sat, 10.00–19.00 Sun Water bus to Rialto).

USEFUL SHOPPING PHRASES

What time do the shops open/close?
A che ora aprono/chiudono i negozi?
Ah keh awra ahprawnaw/kewdawnaw ee nehgotsee?

How much is this?
Quant'è?
Kwahnteh?

Can I try this on?
Posso provarlo?
Pawssaw prawvarrlaw?

My size is ...
La mia taglia è ...
Lah meeyah tahlyah eh ...

I'll take this one, thank you
Prenderò questo, grazie
Prehndehroh kwehstaw, grahtsyeh

Can you show me the one in the window/this one?
Può mostrarmi quello in vetrina/questo?
Poohoh mawstrahrmee kwehllaw een vehtreenah/kwehstaw?

This is too large/small/expensive
Questo è troppo grande/troppo piccolo/troppo caro
Kwehstaw eh tropaw grahndeh/tropaw peekawlaw/tropaw kahraw

The most colourful food market is at the **Rialto Bridge** (🕒 07.30–13.00 Mon–Sat). On the San Polo side of the bridge are stalls selling clothes, leather goods and souvenirs. There is a quieter food market in **Via Garibaldi** in the Castello district (🕒 08.00–12.30 Mon–Sat 🚤 Water bus to Giardini), and a regular market in Rio Terra di San Leonardo in **Cannaregio** (🕒 08.00–12.30 Mon–Sat 🚤 Water bus to San Marcuola or Guglie).

Eating & drinking

There is a huge choice of places to eat and drink in Venice, ranging from ordinary bars and cafés to *bacari* (casual wine bars which serve tapas-style snacks called *cichetti*), more sophisticated *enoteche* (wine bars with more elaborate food), simple trattorias and *osterias*, plus the more formal *ristorante*. You will also find pizzerias, *gelaterie* (ice-cream parlours), tea shops, bakeries, and some excellent cake and pastry shops.

This huge choice of eateries, though, makes it all the more important to pick carefully in order to get a good meal at a reasonable price. Most restaurants near St Mark's Square cater solely for the tourist industry and as a general rule, the closer you are to this area the pricier a meal or a drink will be. Cheaper and better-quality food and wine can often be found in the outlying areas such as Cannaregio (see page 106), Castello (see page 60), and San Polo and Santa Croce (see page 94).

Upmarket hotel restaurants are usually a good bet and can often be less expensive than what appears to be a more casual place. Hotel restaurants also stay open on Sunday and Monday evenings, when many other establishments are closed.

Picnicking on the mini-pizzas, panini (toasted sandwiches), *tramezzini* (regular sandwiches) and other snacks you can buy

PRICE CATEGORIES

Based on the average cost of a three-course evening meal for one person, excluding drinks.

£ up to €35   ££ €35–70   £££ over €70

LOCAL SPECIALITIES & WINE

There are many tasty local specialities in Venice, particularly fish and seafood. Try *anguilla* (eel), *baccalà* (a salt cod dip), *folpi* (baby octopus), *granchio* (crab), *granseola* (spider crab), *sarde in soar* (sardines marinated with onions, pine nuts, raisins and vinegar) or, for a more filling meal, *risotto di mare* or *in nero* (seafood risotto or risotto with squid ink).

If you prefer meat, there is some excellent carpaccio (raw, lean, thinly sliced fillet of beef), *prosciutto San Daniele* (local ham), *fegato alla veneziana* (calves' liver and onions) and *tripa* (tripe, usually served with onions). Common pre-dinner snacks are *acciuge* (anchovies) or *boveleti* (small snails). You can nibble on these while enjoying a *spritz*, a favourite Venetian aperitif consisting of white wine, Campari and soda.

Local wine from the Veneto region, the hinterland behind Venice, is good quality and generally better value than imported varieties. Look out for Valpolicella (a full-bodied red sometimes drunk chilled), Bardolino (another robust red which goes well with meat), Soave (a smooth white), Raboso (a warming, tannic red) and Valadige (red, white or rosé). Wines labelled *superiore* or *classico* tend to be reliable. The region's trademark light sparkling wine, Prosecco, is normally drunk as an aperitif.

Grappa is a strong brandy drunk after dinner and the other local liqueur of choice is the sweet, almond-flavoured Amaretto. Ask your waiter for advice on the several excellent local dessert wines.

in cafés and bakeries is pleasant along the Zattere, by the Giudecca Canal (see page 80). Picnicking in most other areas is frowned on, however, and there are few benches or quiet areas in which to sit.

Many restaurants add an often hefty cover charge to the bill on top of the price of the meal – check before sitting down. A service charge is usually included in the price so it is normal simply to round up the bill to the nearest euro. When service is specifically not included, a tip of ten per cent is fine.

If you visit in peak season and plan to eat in a particular restaurant, make sure you book in advance. If you visit in low season, be aware that some restaurants and bars may be closed.

● *Enjoying an alfresco meal in Campo del Piovan*

ℹ️ Italy now has some of the strictest anti-smoking laws in Europe. Smoking in public buildings or enclosed spaces such as restaurants and bars is strictly forbidden except at outside tables and in designated smoking rooms.

USEFUL DINING PHRASES

I would like a table for ... people
Vorrei un tavolo per ... persone
Vawrray oon tahvawlaw pehr ... perrsawneh

Waiter/Waitress!
Cameriere/Cameriera!
Cahmehryereh/Cahmehryera!

May I have the bill, please?
Mi dà il conto, per favore?
Mee dah eel cawntaw, pehr fahvohreh?

Could I have it well-cooked/medium/rare, please?
Potrei averlo ben cotto/mediamente cotto/poco cotto, per favore?
Pawtray ahvehrlaw behn cawtaw/mehdeeyahmehnteh cawtaw/pawcaw cawtaw, pehr fahvohreh?

I am a vegetarian. Does this contain meat?
Sono vegetariano/vegetariana. Contiene carne?
Sawnaw vejetahreeahnaw/vejetahreeahnah. Contyehneh kahrneh?

Entertainment & nightlife

Carnival excepted, Venice's nightlife tends to be relaxed and quiet. Lazy dinners and evening strolls are more popular than loud music and wild dancing, and many bars and cafés close by 22.00 or earlier. Restaurants tend to stop serving at 22.30 or 23.00. For late-night activity, head for Campo Santa Margherita, Campo Santo Stefano, Campo San Polo, Fondamenta della Misericordia and Campo San Barnaba. Some upmarket restaurants have bars that stay open late. Strict legislation regarding noise levels means that live and open-air

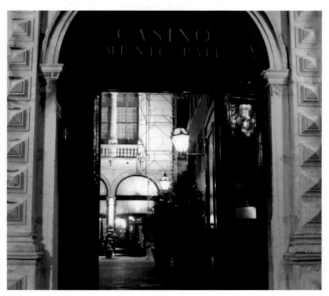

● *The Casinò di Venezia (see page 118)*

music events are not common in the city. Look out for posters advertising classical concerts in churches instead.

Venice's **International Film Festival** in late August and early September (see page 122) draws hordes of film stars and cinema lovers to the Lido and is one time when Venice becomes much more lively than usual. For a quieter cinema event go for the **Circuito Off Venice International Short Film Festival** (see page 10), held around the same time on the tiny island of San Servolo.

In addition, every evening in summer there are open-air film screenings in Campo San Polo (🕐 041 524 4347 🕐 21.00 ❶ Most films are in Italian, except during the Venice Film Festival ❶ Admission charge). The Circuito Cinema film library occasionally screens films in the original language (🅐 Santa Croce 1991, Salizada San Stae 🕐 041 524 1342 🅦 www.comune.venezia.it/cinema). If you are on the Lido, try the **Multisala Astra** (🅐 Via Corfù 9, Lido 🕐 041 526 5736 🅝 Water bus to Lido).

TICKETS & LISTINGS INFORMATION

For detailed listings of upcoming concerts visit 🅦 www.turismovenezia.it

A good fortnightly listings publication in Italian and English is *Un Ospite di Venezia*, available free from hotels and tourist offices or online at 🅦 www.unospitedivenezia.it. For jazz, check 🅦 www.caligola.it

Tickets for most events are available from **ACTV-Vela** 🅐 Santa Croce 509, Piazzale Roma 🕐 07.00–21.00 daily or 🅐 Tronchetto boat terminus 🕐 08.00–18.30 Mon–Sat, closed Sun. Call 🕐 041 2424 or see 🅦 www.hellovenezia.com

Sport & relaxation

SPECTATOR SPORTS

Football Venice's football club Unione Venezia play at **Stadio PL Penzo** in Sant'Elena (⊕ Viale Sant'Elena ⊕ Games Sat & Sun, Sept–June ⊕ Water bus to Sant'Elena). For tickets contact **HelloVenezia** (⊕ 041 2424 ⊕ www.hellovenezia.com).

PARTICIPATION SPORTS

Cycling Cycling is popular on the Lido. For bicycle hire try **Lido On Bike** (⊕ Gran Viale 21B ⊕ 041 526 8019 ⊕ www.lidoonbike.it) or **Giorgio Barberi** (⊕ Gran Viale 79A ⊕ 041 526 1490).

Golf The **Circolo Golf Venezia** on the Lido has beaches and a golf club (⊕ Strada Vecchia 1 ⊕ 041 731 333 ⊕ www.circologolfvenezia.it ⊕ Water bus to Lido).

Gym Try the **Palestra International Club** (⊕ Sotoportego dei Amai ⊕ 041 528 9830 ⊕ Water bus to Rialto) or the **Eutonia Club** (⊕ Dorsoduro, Calle Renier ⊕ 041 522 8618 ⊕ www.eutoniaclub.net (Italian only) ⊕ Water bus to Ca' Rezzonico).

Rowing You can try your hand at rowing – and even participate in the local regattas – at one of Venice's rowing clubs. For lessons contact **Reale Società Canottieri Bucintoro** (⊕ Dorsoduro 263, Zattere ⊕ 041 520 5630 ⊕ www.bucintoro.org).

Swimming For a luxurious hotel swimming pool and spa, visit the **Cipriani** on the island of Giudecca or the rooftop pool of the Hilton Molino Stucky (⊕ Giudecca 10 ⊕ 041 520 7745 www.hotelcipriani.it Water bus to Zitelle). There are also three public pools: **Centro Sportivo Sant'Alvise** (Calle del Capitello, Campo Sant'Alvise 041 715 650 www.ilcentrosantalvise.com Water bus to Sant'Alvise), **Piscina Comunale Sacca Fisola** on the island of Giudecca (Giudecca, San Biagio-sacca Fisola 041 528 5430 www.rarinantesvenezia.it Water bus to Sacca Fisola) and **Piscina Ca' Bianca** (Via Sandro Gallo, Lido 041 526 2222 Water bus to Lido Opening times vary). Public pools require swimmers to wear caps and flip-flops.

Tennis You can play tennis and rent racquets at **Tennis Club Ca' del Moro** on the Lido (Via Ferruccio Parri 6 041 770 965 www.tennisclubcadelmoro.it 08.30–20.30 Mon–Fri, 08.30–20.00 Sat & Sun Water bus to Lido then Bus: V). The club also has a gym and swimming pool.

RELAXATION
Centro Benessere in the Cipriani hotel offers massage, skincare, hot stones, manicures and a hairdresser. Open to non-hotel guests (Giudecca 10 041 240 8016 www.hotelcipriani.it Water bus to Zitelle).

● *Relaxing in a gondola*

Accommodation

Staying in one of Venice's many upmarket hotels or traditional canal-side guesthouses can be a great experience but is also expensive. As a general rule, the closer you stay to St Mark's Square or the Grand Canal, the more you will pay. You can often find good deals through tour operators or websites, particularly if you book well in advance, avoid peak season and visit during the week rather than at the weekend.

Some hotels include a continental or buffet breakfast in their rates but others charge a hefty supplement so do check before booking.

For more information see the helpful Venice tourist information website: Ⓦ www.turismovenezia.it

HOTELS
Agli Alboretti £–££ Popular hotel near the Accademia with a good restaurant and pleasant rooms. Ⓐ Dorsoduro 882, Rio Terra Foscarini Ⓣ 041 523 0058 Ⓦ www.aglialboretti.com Ⓦ Water bus to Accademia

Hotel Rio £–££ Comfortable, modern hotel run by the owner of the nearby Aciugheta restaurant. Not all rooms have en-suite bathrooms. Ⓐ Castello 4358, Campo Santii Filippo e Giacomo Ⓣ 041 523 4810 Ⓦ www.aciugheta-hotelrio.it Ⓦ Water bus to San Zaccaria

PRICE CATEGORIES
Based on the average price per night for two people sharing a double room. Some rooms, particularly those overlooking canals, may be more expensive.
£ up to €150   ££ €150–250   £££ over €250

Locanda del Ghetto £–££ A small, modest hotel with pleasant rooms.
ⓐ Cannaregio 2892, Campo del Ghetto Nuovo ⓣ 041 275 9292
ⓦ www.locandadelghetto.net ⓝ Water bus to San Marcuola

Locanda San Barnaba £–££ Centrally located hotel with 13 spacious
rooms. ⓐ Dorsoduro 2785–6, Calle del Traghetto ⓣ 041 241 1233
ⓦ www.locanda-sanbarnaba.com ⓝ Water bus to Ca' Rezzonico

Al Ponte Mocenigo ££ On the other side of a private bridge,
this good-value hotel is tastefully decorated and charming.
ⓐ Santa Croce 2063, Fondamenta Rimpeto Mocenigo ⓣ 041 524 4797
ⓦ www.alpontemocenigo.com ⓝ Water bus to San Stae

Ca' Pisani ££ Art Deco style in an old merchant's house near the
Accademia. ⓐ Dorsoduro 979A ⓣ 041 240 1411 ⓦ www.capisanihotel.it
ⓝ Water bus to Accademia

Ca' Vendramin di Santa Fosca ££ Small hotel in an old palazzo near
a quiet canal. ⓐ Cannaregio 2400 ⓣ 041 275 0125 ⓦ www.hotel
cavendramin.it ⓝ Water bus to Ca' d'Oro

La Calcina ££ This charming hotel on the Zattere, overlooking
the Redentore and the Giudecca Canal, also has apartments.
ⓐ Dorsoduro 780, Fondamenta delle Zattere ⓣ 041 520 6466
ⓦ www.lacalcina.com ⓝ Water bus to Zattere

Oltre Il Giardino ££ Intimate, tranquil boutique hotel with a garden,
a 15-minute walk from Rialto Bridge. ⓐ San Polo 2542, Fondamenta
Contarini ⓣ 041 275 0015 ⓦ www.oltreilgiardino-venezia.com
ⓝ Water bus to San Tomà

◆ *The imposing Hilton Molino Stucky on the Giudecca*

Cipriani £££ More a resort than a hotel, located on the island of Giudecca. Swimming pool, spa and other facilities, including three restaurants. ⊖ Giudecca 10 ☎ 041 520 7745 Ⓦ www.hotelcipriani.it Ⓝ Water bus to Zitelle; private launch from St Mark's Square

Danieli £££ One of Venice's most famous hotels in the former home of a doge. Impressive décor and roof terrace. ⊖ Castello 4196, Riva degli Schiavoni ☎ 041 522 6480 Ⓦ www.starwoodhotels.com Ⓝ Water bus to San Zaccaria

Gritti Palace £££ Renowned hotel by the Grand Canal decorated with priceless antiques. ⊖ Campo Santa Maria del Giglio 2467 ☎ 041 794 611 Ⓦ www.hotelgrittipalacevenice.com Ⓝ Water bus to San Zaccaria

Hilton Molino Stucky £££ Set in a converted former flour mill, this hotel offers all the comforts of a luxury hotel in the shell of an industrial building. ⊖ Giudecca 753, Fondamenta San Biagio ☎ 041 272 3311 Ⓦ www.molinostuckyhilton.com Ⓝ Water bus to Palanca; private launch from St Mark's Square and the Zattere by arrangement

B&BS

Al Gallion £ Immaculate 16th-century palazzo tucked away behind Campo San Giacomo dell'Orio. ⊖ Santa Croce 1126, Calle Gallion ☎ 041 524 4743 Ⓦ www.algallion.com Ⓝ Water bus to Riva di Biasio

Ca' Miani £ Owned by French hairdresser Pascal Cariou, this central B&B is stylish and tranquil. ⊖ San Marco 2865, Calle del Frutarol ☎ 041 241 1868 Ⓝ Water bus to San Samuele

Al Sole ££ Beautifully restored 14th-century palace. Near the station and Piazzale Roma. ➌ Santa Croce 136, Fondamenta Minotto ➊ 041 244 0328 Ⓦ www.alsolehotels.com Ⓝ Waterbus to Piazzale Roma

Ca' Della Corte ££ A finely decorated 16th-century house with a courtyard. Rooms are bright and spacious. ➌ Dorsoduro 3560, Corte Surian ➊ 041 715 877 Ⓦ www.cadellacorte.com Ⓝ Water bus to Piazzale Roma

HOSTELS

Most hostels have double rooms as well as larger dormitories and charge around €25–50 per room per night.

Casa Santa Dorotea £ ➌ Cannaregio 2927 ➊ 041 717 022 Ⓝ Water bus to Guglie

Residenza Universitaria San Tomà £ ➌ San Polo 2846 ➊ 041 275 0930 Ⓦ www.esuvenezia.it Ⓝ Water bus to San Tomà

⬥ *Classic Venetian style at the Danieli hotel*

THE BEST OF VENICE

Make the most of a short trip to Venice by fitting in as many as possible of its fantastic sights and attractions, but take the time to relax and enjoy the city's special atmosphere as well.

TOP 10 ATTRACTIONS

- **St Mark's Basilica** The oldest and most famous building in Venice is part of the city's soul (see page 60).

- **Boat trips on the canals** Take a water bus from the airport, Lido or islands or splash out on a water taxi or gondola ride. One of the best ways to travel around Venice, see its impressive buildings and churches and relive its history (see page 55).

- **Piazza San Marco & the Campanile** The heart of the city, with museums and shopping all around. You can get great views of Venice from the top of the Campanile, or bell tower (see pages 62 & 65).

- **Accademia Gallery** The place to see the works of the city's greatest artists (see page 85).

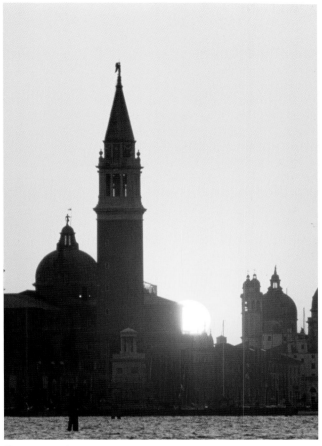

▲ *The magic of sunset in venice*

When it rains

When it rains in Venice – which it often does – you'll see a different but no less fascinating side of the city. Instead of sitting outside a café in one of the squares, soak up the special atmosphere indoors. Try the Caffè Florian in St Mark's Square (see page 62) with its wood panelling and mirrored interiors, or the lushly decorated Harry's Bar (see page 76).

Rain means you can safely spend longer admiring and appreciating the magnificent works of art in churches and museums. The Basilica of San Marco (see page 60) and the Palazzo Ducale (see page 66) should certainly feature on any rainy day itinerary. Shopping for arts, crafts and designer goods can also be rewarding, and the Rialto market buzzes whatever the weather. A ride in a water bus or water taxi under cover will give you a different perspective on the buildings you see – and you will spend less time photographing and more time simply looking.

Venice's nightlife tends to be quiet and based indoors in restaurants, theatres or concert halls, so rain shouldn't make too much difference to your evening entertainment.

It can rain at any time of the year in Venice and there are occasional heavy thunderstorms in summer, so do come prepared with umbrellas, raincoats and strong walking shoes whenever you visit. A look at ⓦ www.weather.com or ⓦ www.bbc.co.uk/weather will let you know what to expect. Thankfully, rain showers do not tend to last long and in summer the streets will dry very quickly.

IF YOU GET LOST, TRY ...

Excuse me, do you speak English?
Mi scusi, parla inglese?
Mee skoozee, pahrlah eenglehzeh?
**Is this the right way to the old town/the city centre/the
tourist office/the station/the bus station?**
È questa la strada per la città vecchia/per il centro città/
per l'ufficio informazioni turistiche/per la stazione ferroviaria/
per la stazione degli autobus?
*Eh kwehstah lah strahda pehr lah cheetta vehkyah/
pehr eel chentraw cheetta/pehr looffeechaw
eenforrmahtsyawnee ṫooreesteekeh/pehr lah statsyoneh
fehrohveeahreeyah/pehr lah statsyoneh delee ahootawboos?*

a space in the **ASM car park** (🅐 Santa Croce 496, Piazzale Roma
🅣 041 272 7211 🅦 www.asmvenezia.it) or the **Venezia Tronchetto Parking**
(🅐 Isola Nova de Tronchetto 1 🅣 041 520 7555 🅦 www.veniceparking.it).

If you do have a car, it is best to take the ferry and stay on the
Lido, where travel and parking are easier. Regular ferries run from
Tronchetto to the San Nicolò ferry terminal on the Lido. Contact
ACTV (🅣 041 2424 🅦 www.actv.it) for more information.

There is now a people mover connecting Tronchetto and
Piazzale Roma.

FINDING YOUR FEET
The centre of Venice is entirely pedestrianised so your transport
options are limited to walking or catching a water taxi or bus. You

will soon get used to this, but take care when walking along canals and when boarding waterborne transport. Wear sensible shoes and avoid carrying heavy luggage.

The Venetian dialect is a variant of standard Italian so some street names and signs may be slightly different to those on the map. *Terra*, for example, is often written as *terà*. *Campo* refers to a small square and a *fondamenta* (sometimes *fondamente*) is a road running along a canal.

ORIENTATION

The very things that make Venice attractive – its warren of small canals, its bridges, its passageways – can also make it confusing. It is a good idea to get hold of a detailed map with a street index from the tourist office. There is an excellent interactive map on Ⓦ www.veniceonline.it

Piazza San Marco, or St Mark's Square, is the largest square in the city. From here you can easily reach many parts of the city on foot, with major landmarks such as Rialto, to the northwest, and Accademia, to the west, clearly signposted. The Grand Canal, spanned by three bridges, snakes southwest through Venice in an

ADDRESSES

Buildings in Venice are numbered according to *sestiere* (district) rather than street. There are six districts: San Marco, Castello, Cannaregio, San Polo, Santa Croce and Dorsoduro. Addresses are usually written with house or building number and district only, eg San Polo 1234, which can make it difficult to find your destination. The street name is given wherever possible in this guide.

inverted 'S' from Piazzale Roma to the huge Baroque church of
Santa Maria della Salute.

GETTING AROUND

Vaporetti (water buses) are run by ACTV (🅐 Offices at Piazzale Roma
in Santa Croce, and Santa Maria Elisabetta on the Lido ☎ 041 2424
🅦 www.actv.it) and are the main form of transport for both locals
and visitors. The buses zigzag along the Grand Canal and other
routes, stopping at alternate banks. Be aware that buses heading
in both directions use the same stops.

Buses are regular and reliable, with the next departure time
displayed on electronic screens at bus stations and a timetable
available from the website. There is space for around 200 people on
a water bus. Access is step-free so unless it is very crowded there is
usually no problem for disabled travellers or those with prams or
heavy luggage.

The most useful buses are Nos 1 and 2, which take around
30 minutes to travel up and down the Grand Canal. Several buses travel

⬤ Water taxis are convenient, but expensive

A Communicarta
Style 45 design
© Communicarta Ltd, 2011 UDN.6d
Map user Ref:WZFG/PG/VCE/2010/40

Morning service direction: A*
Afternoon service direction: B*

**Venezia Mestre &
Inter-City destinations**

Tre Archi

S. Alvise
Madonna
dell'Orto

41 42
51 52

CANNAREGIO

Crea

Guglie

S. Marcuola
Casinò

Ca' d'Oro

Tronchetto

2 2
N N

**Venezia
S. Lucia**

Ferrovia

Riva de
Biasio

SAN
POLO

S. Stae

Rialto
Mercato

Canal Grande

S. Silvestro

P.le Roma
(S. Chiaro): N & 2
(Parisi): 1, 41, 51, 61
(Scomenzera): 42, 52 & DM

S. Toma'

S. Angelo

SAN
MARCO

S. Samuele

2 2

**SANTA
CROCE**

Ca' Rezzonico

San Marco
(Vallaresso)

S. Marta

Accademia

S. Maria
del Giglio

S. Basilio

62 61

Zattere

Spirito
Santo ~

Salute

DORSODURO

42 41

52 51

Sacca
Fisola

Palanca

Zitelle

LA GIUDECCA

Redentore

LA GIUDECCA

Standard routes
— 1
— 2 (10 minute frequency)
— 2 (20 minute frequency)
— 13
— 41 & 42
— 51 & 52
— 61 & 62
— DM (Diretto Murano)
— LN (Laguna Nord)
— N (Night)
— T (Traghetto Torcello)

2 Route
starting point

2 Route
terminating point

* Weekdays only

** Stop by request only

~ 09.00-20.34, Weekdays only

Summer only
= = = 2
= = = 5 (10:15 - 16:54)
= = = 20

up the smaller canals or to the islands. A limited night-bus service operates after midnight.

Single tickets lasting one hour can be bought in advance from an ACTV office or newsagent, at some boat stops, or on board. You can also purchase more economical one-day or three-day tickets that allow unlimited travel. The Venice Card (see page 22) includes unlimited public transport within the city. If you buy it in advance or at the airport, it can also include the Alilaguna airport transfer boat.

Motoscafi (water taxis) take up to 12 passengers. Taxi ranks are situated at Piazzale Roma, Santa Lucia railway station, near the Rialto water-bus stop, next to St Mark's Square, at the Valaresso water-bus stop and at Giardini ex Reali. You can also hail water taxis or order one from your hotel, although hotels often charge a ten per cent booking fee. Even short journeys can be very expensive, with a minimum charge of €70 and a €10 surcharge after midnight, and must be paid for in cash. Always confirm a price with the driver before boarding. See Ⓦ www.venezianamotoscafi.it for more information.

There are over four hundred bridges in Venice but only three over the Grand Canal. A fourth 'Calatrava' bridge has been built, linking Piazzale Roma and the railway station. To cross the Grand Canal you can take a traghetto, which costs €0.50 per person per crossing with standing room only.

Car hire

All car-hire offices are situated at the Piazzale Roma bus terminal.
Avis Ⓣ 041 523 7377 Ⓦ www.avisautonoleggio.it
Europcar Ⓣ 041 523 8616 Ⓦ www.europcar.it
Hertz Ⓣ 041 528 4091 Ⓦ www.hertz.com

▶ *The Punta della Dogana and St Mark's Campanile*

THE CITY OF
Venice

San Marco & Castello

Piazza San Marco (St Mark's Square) was described by Napoleon as 'the drawing room of Europe'. It has been the heart of the city for more than a millennium and is packed with fascinating buildings. The Castello district to the east is usually quieter than other central areas and is worth a visit for its churches of Santa Maria Formosa (see page 69) and Santi Giovanni e Paolo (see page 69). If you need a break from sightseeing, pop into the small **Giardinetti Reali** (Royal Gardens ⏰ 09.00–18.00 daily), originally designed for Napoleon. Or head for the **Giardini Pubblici** (Public Gardens ⓐ Castello, Viale dei Giardini Pubblici ⏰ 08.30–20.00 daily (summer); 08.30–17.30 daily (winter) Ⓦ Water bus to Giardini), the main site of the Biennale festival and one of Venice's few green spaces. It is a tranquil area and a good place to take a break in the shade away from the crowds. For some liquid refreshment go for a drink in the reputed **Hotel Danieli** (ⓐ Castello 4196, Riva degli Schiavoni ☎ 041 522 6480 Ⓦ www.starwoodhotels.com ⏰ Roof terrace bar: 15.00–18.00 daily; lobby bar: 09.30–01.00 daily Ⓦ Water bus to San Zaccaria) and gaze down at the lagoon from the roof terrace.

SIGHTS & ATTRACTIONS

Basilica di San Marco (St Mark's Basilica)

This stunning basilica was originally constructed in the 9th century to house the remains of St Mark, Venice's patron saint, and used to be the private chapel of the doges. What you see today mostly dates from the end of the 11th century. The exterior mosaics date mostly from the 17th and 18th centuries, with only one 13th-century original over the north door.

AROUND PIAZZA SAN MARCO

At the eastern end of Piazza San Marco is the Basilica di San Marco (St Mark's Basilica). Next to it is the Palazzo Ducale (Doge's Palace) and opposite is the Campanile (Bell Tower) from which you can get excellent views of the city.

At the northern end is the Procuratie Vecchie, originally dating from the 12th century, but rebuilt after a fire in the 16th century. It used to house the offices of Venice's powerful magistrates and now contains the well-known **Quadri** café (🅐 San Marco 121, Piazza San Marco ☎ 041 522 2105 Ⓦ www.quadrivenice.com 🕐 09.30–00.30 daily (Apr–Oct); 09.00–23.30 Tues–Sun, closed Mon (Nov–Mar)), which dates back to 1775. Just along from the Quadri is the Torre dell'Orologio, Venice's heavily embellished Renaissance clock tower. The arch beneath it leads to the Mercerie, Venice's main shopping area.

On the south side of the square is the legendary **Caffè Florian** (🅐 San Marco 57, Piazza San Marco ☎ 041 520 5641 Ⓦ www.caffeflorian.com 🕐 10.00–24.00 daily (May–mid-Oct); 10.00–23.00 Fri & Sat, 10.00–21.00 Sun–Thur (mid-Oct–Apr)), with its classic wood-panelled and mirrored interiors, originally opened in 1720 as a club for writers and artists. Both the Florian and the Quadri cafés have live classical music and, although expensive, are big tourist draws. It is part of experiencing the atmosphere of St Mark's Square to have a coffee or glass of wine at one of them.

The western end is the newest part of the square and houses the Correr Museum and the Ala Napoleonica.

The building's design is based on a basilica in Constantinople and Byzantine influences are evident in the elaborate domes and in the 4,000 sq m (43,000 sq ft) of mosaics inside.

Built in the shape of a Greek cross, the vast interior contains several chapels, as well as a baptistery, museum and treasury. The treasury contains a stunning collection of Byzantine gold and silver spoils, including chandeliers and chalices. The most spectacular of all is the Pala d'Oro, a gorgeous gold and gem-encrusted altarpiece, made in Constantinople in 976. It used to be covered by the Pala Feriale, a panel painted by Paolo Veneziano and now on display in the basilica.

If you climb the stairway, you'll find four gilded copper horses overlooking the square – a great photo opportunity. The horses, a symbol of Venice, are thought to be Greek or Roman in origin and were part of the plunder brought back from Constantinople in 1204.

⬤ *St Mark's Basilica*

PHOENIX FROM THE FLAMES

To the west of St Mark's Square is the famous 18th-century opera house of La Fenice, which means 'The Phoenix'. The name derives from this legendary animal's cycle of death and rebirth. The opera house burnt down in 1774, was reopened in 1792, but was subsequently destroyed by fire in 1836. Repaired and reopened again, the interior was heavily damaged by yet another fire in 1996. It was eventually fully restored at the end of 2003, with new stages, state-of-the-art equipment and a new roof, and hopefully this time with improved fire protection. Book well in advance for excellent opera, ballet and concert performances. ⓐ San Marco 1965, Campo San Fantin ⓣ 041 2424 Ⓦ www.teatrolafenice.it Ⓝ Water bus to Sant'Angelo

The horses outside the building are replicas but the originals are protected inside the basilica.

The chancel is separated from the rest of the church by a red marble choir screen. You can access it via the San Clemente chapel and it is worth admiring its intricate mosaic depicting St Mark's body being transported to Venice. ⓐ Piazza San Marco ⓣ 041 270 8311 Ⓦ www.basilicasanmarco.it Ⓛ 09.45–17.00 Mon–Sat, 14.00–16.00 Sun (May–Sept); 09.45–16.45 Mon–Sat, 14.00–16.00 Sun (Oct–Apr) Ⓝ Water bus to Valaresso ⓘ Admission charge for treasury, loggia, Museo Marciano, chancel and Pala d'Oro. Main basilica free of charge. Luggage and rucksacks are not allowed in the basilica. You can leave your bags safely at Ateneo San Basso, a three-minute walk to the left of the main entrance (ⓐ Calle San Basso 315A)

SAN MARCO & CASTELLO

Campanile (Bell Tower)

This 100-m (330-ft) red-brick tower is the tallest building in Venice
and a prominent landmark. It was originally built in the 9th century
but took its current shape in 1514. It collapsed in 1902 but was
rebuilt ten years later. You can take a lift to the top and enjoy great
views of the city on a clear day. Go early if possible to avoid long
queues. ❷ Piazza San Marco ❶ 041 270 8311 ⏰ 09.00–19.00 daily
(Easter–June & Oct); 09.00–21.00 (July–Sept); 09.00–15.45 daily
(Nov–Easter); last entry one hour before closing ❷ Water bus to
Valaresso ❶ Admission charge. Opening times may vary depending
on the weather

Ospedale Civile (City Hospital)

The city's main hospital in the Castello district has an astounding
marble façade on account of its previous role as home to one of

⬥ *The Scuola Grande di San Marco serves as the city hospital's façade*

Venice's wealthy philanthropic *scuole* (charitable societies, see page 72) Ask at reception to visit the library on the first floor to see a fine 16th-century carved wooden ceiling and some interesting paintings. The hospital chapel, the Church of San Lazzaro dei Mendicanti, has an early Tintoretto and a Veronese and is also open to the public. The imposing equestrian statue by Verrocchio just outside is of Bartolomeo Colleoni, the 15th-century mercenary commander.

ⓐ Castello 6777, Campo Santi Giovanni e Paolo ❶ 041 529 4111 ❶ Library: 08.30–14.00 Mon–Fri, closed Sat & Sun; chapel: 08.00–12.00 Mon–Sat, 09.00–10.00 Sun ❶ Chapel opening times may vary

Palazzo Ducale (Doge's Palace)

Originally constructed in the 9th century as a fortress but subsequently destroyed by fire, the present Gothic building dates from the 14th and 15th centuries. The building was the seat of the city's government and doges were ceremonially crowned at the top of the Scala dei Giganti (Giants' Staircase).

As you go in, admire the impressive entrance Porta della Carta, leading to a courtyard. Inside, you will find huge and richly decorated chambers, many with fine paintings by masters such as Tintoretto and Veronese. Look out for Tintoretto's *Paradise* in the Sala del Maggiore Consiglio (Hall of the Great Council). The Ponte dei Sospiri (Bridge of Sighs) leads to the prison, which you can also visit.

It is well worth taking a 'Secret Itineraries' tour to appreciate the best of the art on display. You can book the tour up to two days in advance at the palazzo or by phone. It is fun for children as well as adults and there are regular English-language versions of this tour, which last around 90 minutes. ⓐ San Marco 1 ❶ 041 271 5911 ⓦ www.museiciviciveneziani.it ❶ 09.00–19.00 daily (Apr–Oct);

09.00–17.00 daily (Nov–Mar) ⚲ Water bus to Valaresso
🛈 Admission charge

Palazzo Grassi

This neoclassical palazzo on the Grand Canal, one of the last to
be built before the fall of the Venetian Republic, was designed by
Giorgio Massari in 1749 around a large colonnaded courtyard. It was
recently bought by French tycoon François Pinault and the interior
has been remodelled by Japanese architect Tadao Ando. Selections
from Pinault's vast collection of international modern works of art
are on display in the building, along with exhibitions of specially
commissioned work. With around 200 works on show at a time it is an
exciting destination for lovers of modern art. Check the website for
details of current exhibitions. ⓐ San Marco 3231, Campo San
Samuele ⓘ 041 523 1680; booking: 199 139 139 (Italy), 0445 250313
(abroad) ⓦ www.palazzograssi.it ⓛ 10.00–19.00 Wed–Mon, closed
Tues; last entry one hour before closing ⚲ Water bus to San Samuele
🛈 Admission charge

ARSENALE

While you are in Castello take the chance to stroll around the
vast walled Arsenale complex. Dating from the 12th century,
it was once the world's greatest shipyard and essential to
Venice's naval might. It is largely closed to the public as it is
still a naval headquarters but it is worth admiring its imposing
exterior wall. During the Biennale festivals (see page 9) some
of its buildings are opened up as exhibition and theatre spaces
(ⓐ Campo dell'Arsenale ⚲ Water bus to Arsenale).

Piazzetta San Marco

In front of the Doge's Palace is an area called the Piazzetta containing two granite pillars topped with winged lions, the symbol of Venice. Dating from the 12th century, the columns marked the entrance to Venice at a time when you could only arrive at the city by sea. From the Piazzetta you can see the islands of San Giorgio and Giudecca and the church of Santa Maria della Salute at the end of the Grand Canal. The Grand Canal meanders through Venice's streets for around 4 km (2¹/₂ miles) in an 'S' shape and is the city's main artery, with magnificent palazzi and museums along its length.

San Zaccaria

This church dating back to the 9th century is named after St Zacharias, father of John the Baptist, whose remains are allegedly enshrined in the second altar on the right.

The church's impressive façade was designed by Mauro Codussi in 1515. The bell tower was built in the 13th century, and the lower part of the façade is Gothic, dating from the late 15th century. The interior is large and dark, a mixture of Gothic and Renaissance styles, though the crypt was part of the 9th-century church. The walls of the nave are covered with huge late 17th-century Baroque paintings.

The highlight of the church is Giovanni Bellini's *Madonna and Child and Four Saints* (1505), displayed over the second altar on the left. The chapels of St Athanasius and St Tarasius contain several paintings, including works by Tintoretto, Van Dyck, Giandomenico Tiepolo, as well as polyptychs painted by Antonio Vivarini in 1443.
ⓐ Castello 4693, Campo San Zaccaria ❶ 041 522 1257 ◕ 10.00–12.00, 16.00–18.00 Mon–Sat, 16.00–18.00 Sun ◍ Water bus to San Zaccaria ❶ Admission charge for chapels

Santa Maria Formosa

This church, situated in one of the liveliest and largest squares in
Venice, is worth seeing if only for the grotesque faces on the Baroque
bell tower. The present church was designed by Mauro Codussi in
the late 15th century. It has two façades, one facing the canal and
the other facing the square. Inside are works by Palma il Vecchio and
Bartolomeo Vivarini. ③ Castello 5263, Campo Santa Maria Formosa
① 041 275 0462 ⓦ www.chorusvenezia.org ④ 10.00–17.00 Mon–Sat,
closed Sun ② Water bus to San Zaccaria ① Admission charge

Santi Giovanni e Paolo (Church of St John & St Paul)

Also known as San Zanipolo, this church is one of the largest and most
important in the city. It was originally built in the Gothic style for the
Dominicans and consecrated in the early 15th century. The doorway
is one of the earliest examples of the Renaissance style in Venice;
there are other Renaissance features inside along with a Baroque
high altar. Despite this mixture of styles, the church is remarkable
for its general unity. It was second only to St Mark's Basilica in Venice's
public life and contains fine monuments to no fewer than 25 doges.

The Capella del Rosario has paintings by Veronese, and the chapel
of San Domenico a fine ceiling. There is a lovely polyptych (1464) by
Giovanni Bellini at the second altar on the right. ③ Castello 6363,
Campo SS Giovanni e Paolo ① 041 523 5913 ⓦ www.basilicasanti
giovanniepaolo.it ④ 09.00–18.00 Mon–Sat, 13.00–18.00 Sun &
public holidays ② Water bus to Ospedale ① Admission charge

Santo Stefano

Along one side of the lively Campo Santo Stefano, also sometimes
known as the Campo Francesco Morosini after the 17th-century
doge who lived in the square, is the church of Santo Stefano. It is

worth popping in to see its graceful Gothic interior and sumptuous red and white decoration. Built in the 14th and 15th centuries for the Augustinians, its ceiling is in the shape of ship's keel. You can also see works by Tintoretto in the sacristy. ❷ San Marco 2774, Campo Santo Stefano ❶ 041 275 0462 ❿ www.chorusvenezia.org
🕐 10.00–17.00 Mon–Sat, closed Sun ❷ Water bus to San Samuele
❶ Admission charge

CULTURE

Museo Correr & Museo Archeologico
(Correr & Archaeological Museums)

The Correr Museum, a celebration of Venice's rich art and history, is housed in the Procuratie Nuove at the western end of St Mark's Square and entered through the Ala Napoleonica.

The first few rooms contain historical artefacts and works by Antonio Canova (1757–1822), arguably Venice's greatest sculptor. The real treat is on the second floor, where you can wander around the Quaderia picture gallery to get an excellent overview of Venetian art and its development. Look out for Vittore Carpaccio's *Portrait of a Young Man in a Red Hat* and his *Two Venetian Ladies*. There are also paintings here by Jacopo Bellini and his more celebrated sons Giovanni and Gentile.

Your ticket to the Correr Museum also entitles you to visit the Archaeological Museum. It contains Greek, Roman and Babylonian antiquities, including sculptures from Greece and Rome which influenced Venetian artists. ❷ Piazza San Marco 52 ❶ 041 240 5211 ❿ www.museicivicivenezia.it 🕐 09.00–19.00 daily (Apr–Oct); 09.00–17.00 daily (Nov–Mar); last entry one hour before closing ❷ Water bus to Valaresso ❶ Admission charge

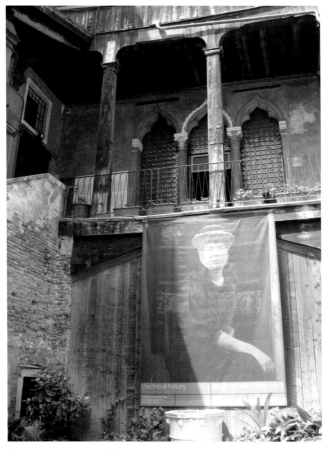

⬤ *The hidden treasure of the Fortuny Museum*

Museo Fortuny (Fortuny Museum)

This crumbling 15th-century house, originally the Palazzo Pesaro degli Orfei, was the home of Spanish fashion designer, painter and photographer Mariano Fortuny. It was left to the city by his widow in 1956 and is currently under long-term restoration work. All three floors remain open throughout the restoration period, which will continue for the foreseeable future, with the museum displaying high-quality photographic and other exhibitions. ⓐ San Marco 3780, Campo San Benedetto ⓣ 041 520 0995 ⓦ www.museicivici veneziani.it ⓛ 10.00–18.00 Wed–Mon, closed Tues ⓦ Water bus to Sant'Angelo ⓘ Admission charge

Museo Storico Navale (Naval History Museum)

Set over four floors in a former granary near the Arsenale, this well-laid-out museum features displays on the history of the Venetian and Italian navies. Other exhibits include a room devoted to the gondola and an impressive collection of seashells. Great for children as well as adults. ⓐ Castello 2148, Riva San Biagio ⓣ 041 244 1399 ⓛ 08.45–13.30 Mon–Fri, 08.45–13.00 Sat, closed Sun ⓦ Water bus to Arsenale ⓘ Admission charge

Scuola di San Giorgio degli Schiavoni

The Venetian *scuole*, mainly founded in the 17th century, were charitable societies formed by laymen who had the same background or profession. Many of these societies were very wealthy and their impressive buildings house some of the city's finest artworks.

The Scuola di San Giorgio degli Schiavoni, founded in the 15th century by Venice's increasingly powerful community of Slavs, is one of the smallest of the many *scuole* in the city but arguably the most enjoyable to visit. The rectangular ground floor is wood panelled and contains a cycle of richly coloured and animated paintings by Vittore Carpaccio depicting the life of St George, St Tryphon and St Jerome. Make sure you look up to admire the wooden ceiling. A staircase lined with paintings leads to the upper hall, also wood panelled, which has a gilded wooden ceiling with oval paintings. ⓐ Castello 3259A, Calle dei Furlani ❶ 041 522 8828 ❷ 14.45–18.00 Mon, 09.15–13.00, 14.45–18.00 Tues–Sat, closed Sun ⓝ Water bus to San Zaccaria ❶ Admission charge

RETAIL THERAPY

Araba Fenice Leading fashion boutique with exclusive designs. ⓐ San Marco 1822, Frezzaria ❶ 041 522 0664 ❷ 10.00–19.30 Mon–Sat, closed Sun ⓝ Water bus to Valaresso

Arnaldo Battois This designer store offers an exclusive selection of garments in luxurious fabrics. ⓐ San Marco 4271, Calle dei Fuseri ❶ 041 528 5944 ⓦ www.arnoldoebattois.com ❷ 10.00–13.00, 15.30–19.30 Mon–Sat, closed Sun ⓝ Water bus to Rialto

Attombri Two local brothers create necklaces and bracelets from antique Venetian glass beads. ⓐ San Marco 2668A, Campo San Maurizio ❶ 041 521 0789 ⓦ www.attombri.com ❷ 09.30– 13.00, 14.30–19.00 Mon–Sat, closed Sun ⓝ Water bus to Giglio

Bevilacqua One of the best shops for fine textiles. ⓐ San Marco 337B, Ponte della Canonica ❶ 041 528 7581 ⓦ www.luigi-bevilacqua.com ❷ 10.00–19.00 Mon–Sat, 09.30–17.00 Sun ⓝ Water bus to Valaresso

Guess Jeans This swish new chain store holds the complete Guess range for men and women. ⓐ San Marco 4596, Calle del Carbon ⓣ 041 241 1494 ⓦ www.guess.eu ⓛ 09.30–19.30 Mon–Sat, 11.00–19.30 Sun ⓝ Water bus to Rialto

Ottico Fabbricatore Stylish store selling designer eyewear, cashmere and leather bags. ⓐ San Marco 4773, Calle dell'Ovo ⓣ 041 522 5263 ⓦ www.otticofabbricatore.com ⓛ 09.00–12.30, 15.30–19.30 Mon–Sat, closed Sun ⓝ Water bus to Rialto

Papier Mâché This workshop produces unusual paper creations using traditional techniques. ⓐ Castello 5175, Calle Lunga Santa Maria Formosa ⓣ 041 522 9995 ⓦ www.papiermache.it ⓛ 09.00–19.30 Mon–Sat, 10.00–19.00 Sun ⓝ Water bus to Rialto

🔺 *Window-shopping in Venice's fashionable Mercerie street*

Il Papiro Stationery and attractive boxes made of marbled paper.
🅰 San Marco 2764, Calle del Piovan ☎ 041 522 3055 🕐 10.00–20.00
daily 🚤 Water bus to Arsenale and 🅰 Castello 5275, Calle delle Bande
☎ 041 522 3648 🕐 10.30–19.00 daily 🚤 Water bus to Rialto

Pelletteria Silvia Beautifully crafted shoes and quality bags in the
softest leather and suede. 🅰 Castello 5540, Salizzada San Lio ☎ 041
523 8568 🕐 09.00–19.30 Mon–Sat, closed Sun 🚤 Water bus to Rialto

Il Prato One of the city's best glass shops. 🅰 San Marco 2457, Calle de
le Ostreghe ☎ 041 523 1148 🕐 10.00–19.30 Mon–Sat, 11.00–19.00 Sun
🌐 www.ilpratovenezia.net 🚤 Water bus to Giglio

Venetia Studium High-quality silk lamps and soft furnishings.
🅰 San Marco 2403, Calle Larga San Marco ☎ 041 522 9281 🌐 www.
venetiastudium.com 🕐 10.00–19.40 Mon–Sat, 10.30–18.00 Sun
🚤 Water bus to Valaresso

TAKING A BREAK

All'Angolo £ ❶ Popular café serving sandwiches and snacks. 🅰 San
Marco 3464, Campo Santo Stefano ☎ 041 522 0710 🕐 06.30–23.00
daily (summer); 06.30–21.00 daily (winter) 🚤 Water bus to
San Samuele

Andrea Zanin £ ❷ Owner Andrea produces delectable pastries,
with miniature versions for the calorie-conscious. Small pizzas and
savoury pastries also available. 🅰 San Marco 4589, Campo San Luca
☎ 041 522 4803 🕐 07.30–20.00 Mon–Sat, 10.30–19.30 Sun
🚤 Water bus to Rialto

Leon Bianco £ ❸ Good-value hot dishes and traditional *cichetti* (snacks). ⓐ San Marco 4153, Salizzada San Luca ❶ 340 892 0803 ⓦ www.osterialeonbianco.it ⓛ 12.00–15.00, 19.00–22.00 Mon–Sat, closed Sun ⓝ Water bus to Rialto

Teamo £ ❹ Hip new lounge bar with an excellent range of light meals and wines. ⓐ San Marco 3795, Rio Terra della Mandola ❶ 347 366 5016 ⓦ www.teamo.it ⓛ 08.00–22.00 Mon–Sat, closed Sun ⓝ Water bus to Sant'Angelo

All'Aciugheta £–££ ❺ Restaurant, bar and café set in a tiny square, offering wine, snacks, pizzas and full meals. ⓐ Castello 4357, Campo Santi Fillipo e Giacomo ❶ 041 522 4292 ⓛ 11.00–24.00 daily ⓝ Water bus to San Zaccaria

Harry's Bar £££ ❻ The place to see and be seen. Food is expensive but good. Pop in for an impeccably served sandwich or splash out on a cocktail. ⓐ San Marco 1323, Calle Vallaresso ❶ 041 528 57 77 ⓦ www.cipriani.com ⓛ 10.30–23.00 daily ⓝ Water bus to Valaresso

AFTER DARK

The area around San Marco is surprisingly quiet late in the evening, and Castello is emptier still. Most restaurants close by 22.00.

RESTAURANTS & WINE BARS

Bandierette £ ❼ Excellent-value lunch or dinner in this low-key restaurant. ⓐ Castello 6671, Barbaria delle Tole ❶ 041 522 0619 ⓛ 12.00–14.00 Mon, 12.00–14.00, 19.00–22.00 Wed–Sun, closed Tues ⓦ www.bandierette.it ⓝ Water bus to Ospedale

Cavatappi £ **❽** Wine bar serving tasty snacks during the day and fuller meals in the evening. **❸** San Marco 525, Campo della Guerra **❶** 041 296 0252 **❹** 10.00–21.00 Tues–Thur, 10.00–24.00 Fri & Sat, 10.00–18.00 Sun, closed Mon **❻** Water bus to Valaresso

A la Campana £–££ **❾** Good traditional food in a rustic atmosphere. Popular with locals for both lunch and dinner. **❸** San Marco 4720, Calle dei Fabbri **❶** 041 528 5170 **❹** 12.00–15.00, 19.00–22.00 Mon–Sat, closed Sun **❻** Water bus to Rialto

Alla Botte £–££ **❿** Lively wine bar with a restaurant serving simple, reasonably priced pasta and local dishes. You can also get snacks at the bar all day. **❸** San Marco 5482, Campo San Bartolomeo **❶** 041 520 9775 **❹** 12.00–15.00 Wed, 12.00–15.00, 19.00–23.00 Thur–Tues (Aug–June); closed July **❻** Water bus to Rialto

● *Soak up the atmosphere in the cafés on St Mark's Square*

Alla Mascareta ££ ⑪ Popular, unpretentious wine bar with simple but tasty food. One of the few late-opening bars around. 🅐 Castello 5183, Calle Lunga Santa Maria Formosa 🅣 041 523 0744 🅛 19.00–02.00 Fri–Tues, closed Wed & Thur 🅦 Water bus to San Zaccaria

Alle Testiere ££ ⑫ Specialises in fish and seafood subtly flavoured with herbs and spices. 🅐 Castello 5801, Calle del Mondo Novo 🅣 041 522 7220 🅦 www.osterialletestiere.it 🅛 12.00–14.30, 19.00–23.00 Tues–Sat, closed Sun & Mon 🅦 Water bus to San Zaccaria

Bacaro ££ ⑬ A fashionable late-opening bar and restaurant, with pricey but good-quality food. 🅐 San Marco 1345, Salizada San Moisè 🅣 041 296 0687 🅛 11.00–02.00 Mon–Sat, closed Sun 🅦 Water bus to Valaresso

Osteria San Marco ££ ⑭ Compact eatery with exemplary wine list. 🅐 San Marco 1610, Frezzeria 🅣 041 528 5242 🅦 www.osteria sanmarco.it 🅛 12.30–23.00 Mon–Sat, closed Sun 🅦 Water bus to San Marco

Vino Vino ££ ⑮ This wine bar is attached to Antico Martini, one of Venice's oldest restaurants, and has established itself as one of Venice's best for both food and wine. 🅐 San Marco 2007A, Calle della Veste 🅣 041 241 7688 🅦 www.vinovinowinebar.com 🅛 11.30–23.30 daily 🅦 Water bus to Valaresso or Giglio

Acqua Pazza ££–£££ ⑯ A favoured place for sitting out in the square under awnings. Excellent southern Italian pizzas and pasta but the service receives mixed reports. 🅐 San Marco 3808, Campo Sant'Angelo 🅣 041 277 0688 🅦 www.veniceacquapazza.com

🕐 12.00–14.00, 19.00–22.00 Tues–Sun, closed Mon 🚤 Water bus to Sant'Angelo

Centrale ££–£££ ⑰ Trendy late-opening lounge bar and restaurant with stylish décor and low lighting. Regular live music. 📍 San Marco 1659B, Piscina Frezzeria ☎ 041 296 0664 🕐 18.30–02.00 daily 🌐 www.centrale-lounge.com 🚤 Water bus to Valaresso

Al Covo £££ ⑱ One of the best restaurants in Venice, famed for its excellent fish and meat dishes served in comfortable surroundings. 📍 Castello 3968, Campiello della Pescaria ☎ 041 522 3812 🌐 www.ristorantealcovo.com 🕐 12.45–14.00, 19.30–22.00 Fri–Tues, closed Wed & Thur 🚤 Water bus to Arsenale

La Cusina £££ ⑲ Hotel restaurant on the Grand Canal serving inventive dishes based on fresh local produce, particularly fish. For a romantic meal book the table on the small jetty. 📍 San Marco 2159, Hotel Europa & Regina ☎ 041 240 3759 🌐 www.westineuropa reginavenice.com 🕐 12.30–14.30, 19.30–22.30 daily 🚤 Water bus to Valaresso

ENTERTAINMENT

Two of Venice's best theatres, La Fenice opera house (see page 64) and Teatro Carlo Goldoni (see page 22), are in this area. Otherwise, evening entertainment is based around the restaurants and the orchestras at the Quadri and Florian cafés (see page 62). For late-night cocktails and music, you can try **Bar Aurora** 📍 San Marco 49, Piazza San Marco ☎ 041 528 6405 🕐 08.30–02.00 daily (Mar–Oct); 08.30–02.00 Wed–Mon, closed Tues (Nov–Feb) 🚤 Water bus to Valaresso

Dorsoduro

The popular district of Dorsoduro, just across the Accademia Bridge, contains three of Venice's best museums – the Accademia with its fine collection of Venetian art, the Ca' Rezzonico with its focus on 18th-century Venice and the Peggy Guggenheim Collection of contemporary art. There are also several fine churches. The area is young and lively, filled with students and visitors. Walking along the Grand Canal section of Dorsoduro gives you a different perspective on the magnificent façades of the San Marco side.

Most of the area's sights, small galleries and craft shops are in the eastern part, many lining the Grand Canal. The far western part is a working-class dock area, some of which is now being redeveloped. At the far eastern end of Dorsoduro is the vast 17th-century *dogana*, or customs house, which has now reopened as the Punta della Dogana art gallery.

South of the Grand Canal is the quayside of Zattere, one of the most relaxing and attractive places in Venice in which to have lunch or a drink. Here you get a view of the island of Giudecca and can watch the local rowing clubs practising. Other good places to relax are the Campo Santa Margherita or Campo San Barnaba, two of Venice's liveliest squares.

SIGHTS & ATTRACTIONS

Gesuati (Santa Maria del Rosario)

Walk along the Zattere quayside and pay a quick visit to this striking church, designed by Giorgio Massari and completed in 1735. It faces Palladio's church of Il Redentore on the island of Giudecca (see page 123) and its façade is a deliberate reflection of the other

church. Inside, look out for the theatrical sculptures by Giovanni Morlaiter and for Giambattista Tiepolo's ceiling frescoes.

① Dorsoduro 917, Fondamenta Zattere ai Gesuati **①** 041 523 0625
Ⓦ www.chorusvenezia.org **●** 10.00–17.00 Mon–Sat, closed Sun
Ⓝ Water bus to Zattere **①** Admission charge

San Sebastiano

The 16th-century church of San Sebastiano is the best place to see the sumptuous work of Paolo Veronese (1528–88). The painter moved to Venice as a young man and lived and died near the church, where he was later buried. His luminous ceiling paintings depict the lives of Esther and St Sebastian. The unity of the decoration and the radiance of Veronese's style make the church's interior one of the

⬤ *You can't help but admire Santa Maria della Salute*

most beautiful in Venice. ❷ Dorsoduro 1686, Campo San Sebastiano
❶ 041 275 0462 ⓦ www.chorusvenezia.org ⓛ 10.00–17.00 Mon–Sat,
closed Sun ⓝ Water bus to San Basilio ❶ Admission charge

Santa Maria della Salute

Dominating the entrance to the Grand Canal, this domed church with
its gorgeously carved Baroque façade is an instantly recognisable
symbol of Venice. *Salute* means 'health', and the church was built in
thanksgiving after the end of a terrible plague in 1630 which killed
a third of the city's population. It is the centre of the yearly Festa
della Salute celebrations on 21 November, in which thanks-givers
walk across a temporary pontoon bridge from the Gritti Palace hotel
to the church and street vendors mingle with the crowds selling candy
floss, balloons and votive candles.

The church was designed by architect Baldassare Longhena but
remained unfinished until 1687, five years after Longhena's death.
Given the grandeur of the exterior, the interior is surprisingly
muted, although the marble floor stands out. One altar contains
Titian's *Descent of the Holy Spirit* (1550). The best paintings are in the
sacristy, including Titian's early altarpiece *St Mark Enthroned with
Saints* (1512) and Tintoretto's *Wedding at Cana* (1551). ❷ Campo della
Salute ❶ 041 274 3928 ⓛ 09.00–12.00, 15.00–17.30 daily ⓝ Water bus
to Salute ❶ Admission charge for sacristy

CULTURE

Ca' Rezzonico

Here is the place to get an idea of the splendour in which the richest
Venetians once lived. This Baroque palazzo, designed in 1667 by
Baldassare Longhena for the wealthy Bon family, was subsequently

sold to the wealthy Rezzonico family. It was bought by the son of poet Robert Browning, who died in the house in 1889. It has been a museum since 1936.

The building's splendid decorative features include massive chandeliers, fine carved furniture, tapestries, ceilings painted by Giambattista Tiepolo and frescoes by Giandomenico Tiepolo. The architectural highlight is Giorgio Massari's magnificent ballroom with its gilded wood and *trompe l'œil* paintings.

In the gallery on the second floor are two rare Canaletto paintings along with 18th-century scenes of Venetian life by Francesco Guardi and Pietro Longhi. On the third floor is a reconstructed 18th-century pharmacy. Make sure you take time to admire the view from the

◔ *Take a stroll over the famous Accademia Bridge*

ACCADEMIA BRIDGE
To reach the Accademia from Campo Santo Stefano you will cross a busy wooden bridge known as the Accademia Bridge. Originally built in cast iron in 1854, it was later demolished for being too low. A wooden bridge was erected as a temporary structure in 1932 and replaced with a stronger replica in 1984. Standing on the bridge will give you some great views of the Grand Canal.

upper floors. ❸ Dorsoduro 3136, Fondamenta Rezzonico ❶ 041 241 0100 Ⓦ www.museiciviciveneziani.it ❶ 10.00–18.00 Wed–Mon, closed Tues (Apr–Oct); 10.00–17.00 Wed–Mon, closed Tues (Nov–Mar) ❷ Water bus to Ca' Rezzonico ❶ Admission charge

Galleria dell'Accademia (Accademia Gallery)

The Accademia Gallery is arguably one of the world's greatest art galleries. The building is currently being extended, but most of the 24 rooms should stay open during this time.

The galleries, mostly arranged chronologically, contain early Byzantine-influenced works and slightly later Gothic devotional works including paintings by Paolo Veneziano. Early Renaissance works by Giovanni Bellini and Vittore Carpaccio follow, but the highlight for most visitors is the superb collection of High Renaissance art including paintings by masters such as Titian, Tintoretto, Veronese, Giorgione and Mantegna. Look out for Titian's *St John the Baptist* (1535) and his final *Pietà* (1576), for Veronese's huge *Feast in the House of Levi* (1573) and Tintoretto's dark and dramatic *Translation of the Body of St Mark* (1562) and *Miracle of the Slave* (1548). Other paintings not to miss are

Lorenzo Lotto's sensitive *Portrait of a Gentleman* (1525) and Giorgione's wonderfully enigmatic *The Tempest* (1507).

Artists featured in the rest of the collection are Jacopo Bassano, Giambattista Tiepolo, Canaletto, Carpaccio and Bellini, whose paintings depict Venice in the 16th century. *The Life of St Ursula* (1590–95) by Carpaccio and Titian's outstanding *Presentation of the Virgin* (1538) are two other highlights of the museum. ❸ Dorsoduro 1050, Campo Carita ❶ 041 520 0345 Ⓦ www.gallerieaccademia.org ❶ 09.00–14.00 Mon, 08.15–19.15 Tues–Sun Ⓝ Water bus to Accademia ❶ Admission charge

A GONDOLA TO THE GUGGENHEIM

The Peggy Guggenheim Collection is one of Venice's most popular art museums, containing a fantastic collection of contemporary works. Peggy Guggenheim (1898–1979) moved into the Palazzo Venier dei Leoni on the Grand Canal in 1949. The art collection that she bequeathed contains Cubist works by Braque, Picasso and Leger as well as paintings by Surrealist artists such as Magritte, Dalí and Max Ernst. You can also admire a good collection of works by Paul Klee, Jackson Pollock and other Abstract Expressionists. The museum's most recognisable sculpture, a priapic rider with outstretched arms, is Marino Marini's *Angel of the City*.

The museum also offers visitors excellent views from the terrace, a pleasant sculpture garden, a bookshop and a good café. ❸ Dorsoduro 701, Palazzo Venier dei Leoni ❶ 041 240 5411 Ⓦ www.guggenheim-venice.it ❶ 10.00–18.00 Wed–Mon, closed Tues Ⓝ Water bus to Salute ❶ Admission charge

Punta della Dogana

This contemporary art centre is the latest addition to Venice's burgeoning scene. It holds the permanent collection of François Pinault, who also owns the sister collection in Palazzo Grassi. The building has been beautifully restored by Japanese architect Tadao Ando and offers stunning views of both the Guidecca and the Grand Canal. ⊕ Dorsoduro 2, Campo della Salute ⊕ 199 139 139 (bookings) ⓦ www.palazzograssi.it ⊕ 10.00–19.00 Wed–Mon, closed Tues ⓝ Water bus to Salute ⊕ Admission charge

◆ The Angel of the City, *at the Guggenheim Museum*

San Pantalon

The exterior of this church is mundane, but step inside and be astonished by its remarkable illusionist ceiling depicting *The Martyrdom and Apotheosis of St Pantalon* by Gian Antonio Fumiani. The 40 canvases took Fumiani 24 years to complete from the start of his commission in 1680. ❸ Dorsoduro 3765, Campo San Pantalon ❶ 041 270 2464 ❻ 15.00–18.00 Mon–Sat, closed Sun ❷ Water bus to San Tomà

Scuola Grande dei Carmini

Baldasarre Longhena, famed architect of Santa Maria della Salute, was commissioned by the Carmelite order to build this *scuola* in 1667. The highlights are Giambattista Tiepolo's nine characteristic ceiling paintings. ❸ Dorsoduro 2617, Campo dei Carmini ❶ 041 528 9420 ❾ www.scuolagrandecarmini.it ❻ 09.00–18.00 Mon–Sat, 09.00–16.00 Sun (Apr–Oct); 09.00–16.00 daily (Nov–Mar) ❷ Water bus to Ca' Rezzonico ❶ Admission charge

RETAIL THERAPY

3865 Fashionable women's clothing and accessories. ❸ Dorsoduro 3749, Calle San Pantalon ❶ 041 720 595 ❻ 10.00–19.45 Tues–Sat, closed Sun & Mon ❷ Water bus to San Tomà

Antichita Antique glass beads made into necklaces or bracelets while you wait. ❸ Dorsoduro 1195, Calle della Toletta ❶ 041 522 3159 ❻ 09.30–13.00, 15.30–19.00 Mon–Sat, closed Sun ❷ Water bus to Accademia

Il Canapé Sumptuous fabric and interior design store. ❸ Dorsoduro 3736, Calle San Pantalon ❶ 041 714 264 ❾ www.ilcanape.it ❻ 15.15–19.30

Mon, 09.00–12.45, 15.15–19.30 Tues–Sat, closed Sun 🚤 Water bus to San Tomà

Lanterna Magica Delightful toys and games for all age groups.
📍 Dorsoduro 2808, Campo San Barnaba ☎ 041 523 8313
🕐 09.30–19.30 Mon–Sat, 10.00–19.00 Sun 🚤 Water bus to Ca' Rezzonico

Madera Contemporary tableware and other design objects.
📍 Dorsoduro 2762, Campo San Barnaba ☎ 041 522 4181
🌐 www.maderavenezia.it 🕐 10.30–13.00, 15.30–19.30 Mon–Sat, closed Sun 🚤 Water bus to Ca' Rezzonico

Mondo Novo One of the city's best mask shops. 📍 Dorsoduro 3063, Rio Terra Canal ☎ 041 528 7344 🌐 www.mondonovomaschere.it
🕐 09.00–18.30 Mon–Sat, closed Sun 🚤 Water bus to Ca' Rezzonico

Officina Veneziana A positive Aladdin's Cave of trinkets and baubles.
📍 Dorsoduro 3752A, Calle San Pantalon ☎ 041 720 313 🌐 www.officinaveneziana.com 🕐 10.30–13.00, 15.30–19.00 Mon–Sat, closed Sun 🚤 Water bus to San Tomà

Il Pavone Attractive handmade paper products. 📍 Dorsoduro 721, Fondamenta Venier dei Leoni ☎ 041 523 4517 🕐 09.30–13.30, 14.30–18.30 daily 🚤 Water bus to Salute

TAKING A BREAK

The Zattere is great for relaxing in cafés and is one of the few places in the city where you can picnic. For a more vibrant atmosphere and cheaper food, make your way to the lively Campo Santa Margherita or Campo San Barnaba.

Ai Do Draghi £ ❶ Good sandwiches, salads, wines and beers. Tables outside. ❸ Dorsoduro 3665, Campo Santa Margherita 🕒 07.00–01.00 daily 🚤 Water bus to Ca' Rezzonico

Cantinone Già Schiavi £ ❷ A comprehensive selection of local wines and light bites. ❸ Dorsoduro 992, Ponte San Trovaso 🕿 041 523 0034 🕒 08.00–20.30 Mon–Sat, 09.00–13.30 Sun 🚤 Water bus to Zattere

Da Gino £ ❸ Popular with students, this café is good for sandwiches. ❸ Dorsoduro 853A, Calle Nuova Sant'Agnese 🕿 041 528 5276 🕒 06.00–19.30 Mon–Sat, closed Sun 🚤 Water bus to Accademia

Gelateria Lo Squero £ ❹ Some of the best ice cream in Venice. ❸ Dorsoduro 989, Fondamenta Nani 🕿 347 269 7921 🕒 10.30–20.00 daily 🚤 Water bus to Zattere

Mille Vini £ ❺ Great-value eatery in the heart of Dorsoduro. Great for people-watching. ❸ Dorsoduro 5362, Campo Santa Margherita 🕿 041 522 3436 🕒 10.00–15.00, 17.30–24.00 daily 🚤 Water bus to Ca' Rezzonico

Orange £ ❻ Trendy modern champagne and wine bar with tables outside, popular with students. Good snacks, coffee, cocktails and light meals. ❸ Dorsoduro 3054, Campo Santa Margherita 🕿 041 523 4740 🕒 10.00– 02.00 daily 🚤 Water bus to Ca' Rezzonico

Ai Artisti £–££ ❼ A simple stop for a drink, a Venetian fish dish or plate of pasta. ❸ Dorsoduro 1196A, Fondamenta della Toletta ❶ 041 523 8944 ❾ www.enotecaartisti.com ❷ 12.00–16.00, 19.00–22.00 Mon–Sat, closed Sun ❷ Water bus to Accademia

Enoteca Vinus Venezia £–££ ❽ Elegant establishment serving fine wines and mouthwatering snacks. ❸ Dorsoduro 3961, Campiello San Rocco ❶ 041 243 8875 ❷ 09.30–22.00 Mon–Sat, closed Sun ❷ Water bus to San Tomà

San Basilio ££ ❾ Venetian cuisine with a great view of Giudecca island. ❸ Dorsoduro 1516, Fondamenta Zattere all Ponte Lungo ❶ 041 521 0028 ❷ 10.00–21.30 Tues–Sat, closed Sun & Mon ❷ Water bus to San Basilio

AFTER DARK

The squares of Santa Margherita and San Barnaba and the streets around them are among the few lively parts of Venice after midnight. The quieter Zattere makes for a relaxing post-dinner stroll.

RESTAURANTS

Antico Capon £ ❿ A lively pizzeria with outside tables and pizzas made in a wood oven. ❸ Dorsoduro 3004B, Campo Santa Margherita ❶ 041 528 5292 ❷ 08.00–24.00 daily ❷ Water bus to Ca' Rezzonico

Trattoria Da Silvio £ ⓫ Modern restaurant with a pretty garden offering pizza and pasta. ❸ Dorsoduro 3748/3818, Calle San Pantalon ❶ 041 520 5833 ❷ 12.00–23.00 daily (Mar–Oct); 12.00–23.00 Mon–Sat, closed Sun (Nov–Feb) ❷ Water bus to San Tomà

Avogaria ££ Chic restaurant with outside tables serving traditional southern Italian dishes from Puglia. The bar opens at 07.00. Avogaria also has three charming guest rooms. ⓐ Dorsoduro 1629, Calle d'Avogaria ⓣ 041 296 0491 ⓦ www.avogaria.com ⓛ 11.30–15.00, 19.30–23.00 Wed–Mon, closed Tues ⓝ Water bus to Ca' Rezzonico

Osteria-Enoteca San Barnaba ££ Intimate eatery serving mainly northern Italian meat dishes. Exceptional wine list. ⓐ Dorsoduro, Calle Lunga San Barnaba ⓣ 041 521 2754 ⓛ 12.00–14.30, 19.00–22.30 Thur–Tues, closed Wed ⓝ Water bus to Ca' Rezzonico

Linea d'Ombra ££–£££ Try to get a table on the terrace for fabulous views of Giudecca and San Giorgio. Also pleasant for a pre-lunch or late afternoon drink. ⓐ Dorsoduro 19, Ponte dell'Umiltà ⓣ 041 241 1881 ⓛ 12.00–15.00, 19.00–22.00 Wed–Mon, closed Tues (Feb–Nov); closed Dec & Jan ⓝ Water bus to Zattere or Salute

Ai Gondolieri £££ One of Venice's most elegant restaurants, with rich, tempting food and good wine to match. Pricey but worth it. ⓐ Dorsoduro 336, Ponte del Formager ⓣ 041 528 6396 ⓦ www. aigondolieri.it ⓛ 12.00–15.00, 19.00–22.00 Wed–Mon, closed Tues ⓝ Water bus to Salute

BARS

Blues Cafe Rock and blues, occasionally played live. ⓐ Dorsoduro 3778, Calle de la Scuola ⓣ 348 240 6444 ⓛ 20.00–02.00 Mon–Fri, 10.00–02.00 Sat, 15.00–02.00 Sun ⓝ Water bus to San Tomà

Caffè Rosso Bustling atmosphere and good wine, with live music some evenings. Popular with students. ⓐ Dorsoduro 2963, Campo

Santa Margherita ☎ 041 528 7998 ⓦ www.cafferosso.it ⏰ 07.00–
01.30 Mon–Sat, closed Sun ⓦ Water bus to Ca' Rezzonico

Venice Jazz Club One of the few places in Venice with live music.
ⓐ Fondamenta dei Squero 3102, Ponte dei Pugni ☎ 041 523 2056
ⓦ www.venicejazzclub.com ⏰ 21.00–23.00 Mon, Wed, Fri & Sat,
19.00–21.00 Tues, closed Thur & Sun ⓦ Water bus to Ca' Rezzonico

🔺 *The Baroque Gesuati church (see pages 80–82)*

San Polo & Santa Croce

The adjoining districts of San Polo and Santa Croce, bordered by the northern curve of the Grand Canal, form a lively area which is always buzzing with students. It is fun to get lost wandering around the maze of tiny streets and canals but if you are in a hurry to get to one of the important sights in the area it's best to take water bus No 1 to the nearest stop.

To relax with a coffee, sit in the lively Campo San Polo, the second-biggest square in Venice and at one time a centre for riotous

THE RIALTO MARKET

For a historic shopping experience buy your souvenirs at the markets around the Rialto Bridge. The current structure was designed by Antonio del Ponte, whose surname incidentally means 'bridge', and completed in 1591. The Rialto is naturally one of the highest areas in Venice and was the site of one of the first settlements in the area, allegedly populated as early as the 5th century. It prospered as the trading centre of the city from the beginning of the 12th century.

The markets, mostly on the San Polo side of the Grand Canal, still thrive. There are plenty of stalls selling souvenirs and trinkets but the real treat is the bustling fish and vegetable market to the right of the Rialto Bridge. The produce is brought to the market by barge so get there early to catch the unloading and to see the stalls being laid out at their most colourful and tempting. ◕ 08.00–12.30 Mon–Sat (no fish market Mon), closed Sun ◎ Water bus to Rialto Mercato

◆ *The famous Rialto Bridge*

carnival festivities. It is surrounded by impressive buildings and has an attractive church, as does the quieter nearby square of San Giacomo dell'Orio. The small, leafy gardens of Giardino Papadopoli, near Piazzale Roma (🕐 08.30–20.00 daily (summer); 08.30–17.30 daily (winter)), offer a haven of calm on a hot or busy day.

SIGHTS & ATTRACTIONS

San Polo

Originally built in the Byzantine style in the 9th century, this small church was extensively altered both in the 15th century (Gothic style) and in the 19th century (neoclassical). The bell tower dates from the 14th century. The interior is notable for a luminous cycle of paintings by Giandomenico Tiepolo (1727–1804) as well as work by his more famous father, Gianbattista. You will also find Tintoretto's *Last Supper* and Veronese's *Marriage of the Virgin*. ❸ San Polo 2102, Campo San Polo ☎ 041 275 0462 🌐 www.chorusvenezia.org 🕐 10.00–17.00 Mon–Sat, closed Sun ⓦ Water bus to San Tomà ❶ Admission charge

Santa Maria Gloriosa dei Frari

Built by the Franciscan friars and commonly known simply as Frari, the stark brick exterior of this huge Gothic church gives no indication as to the splendour of the art inside. The current building, in the shape of a Latin cross, dates from the mid-15th century. The bell tower is the second tallest in Venice after the Campanile in St Mark's Square.

The artworks on display include Titian's stunning *Assumption of the Virgin* (1518) dominating the high altar and his *Madonna di Ca' Pesaro* (1526) in the left-hand aisle. Giovanni Bellini's glowing triptych *Madonna Enthroned with Saints* (1488) is in the sacristy on the far right and you can also admire Donatello's wooden statue of John the Baptist (1438). Look out for the highly decorated choir screen, monuments to Titian and to the 15th-century doge Foscari, and the grave of the composer Claudio Monteverdi. ❸ San Polo 3072, Campo dei Frari ☎ 041 275 0462 🌐 www.chorusvenezia.org 🕐 09.00–18.00 Mon–Sat, 13.00–18.00 Sun ⓦ Water bus to San Tomà ❶ Admission charge

CULTURE

Ca' Pesaro (Galleria Internazionale d'Arte Moderna)

This imposing 17th-century Baroque palazzo, built for the wealthy Pesaro family, was the last project undertaken by Venice's great architect Baldassare Longhena. When Longhena died in 1682 the work was taken over by Antonio Gaspari, and the building was finished in 1703. You can get some superb views of the Grand Canal from the upper floors.

● *Stop off at the palatial Ca' Pesaro*

Today it houses two art collections. Most of the building is taken up by a gallery of modern art mostly devoted to 19th- and 20th-century Italian painters but also including works by Miró, Matisse, Kandinsky, Klimt and Chagall. On the upper floors is a collection of oriental art and artefacts featuring Japanese arms and armour, paintings, sculpture, musical instruments, pottery and lacquerwork. ⓐ Santa Croce 2076, Fondamenta Ca' Pesaro ❶ 041 524 0662 ⓦ www.museiciviciveneziani.it ❶ 10.00–17.00 Tues–Sun, closed Mon; last entry one hour before closing ⓝ Water bus to San Stae ❶ Admission charge

Scuola Grande di San Rocco

The opulence of the ornate stone Renaissance façade on this 16th-century *scuola* indicates the wealth of the charitable brotherhood of San Rocco. Set up to help the sick, the association was named in honour of San Rocco (St Roch), patron saint of victims of the plague.

The building's most stirring feature is the interior, covered floor to ceiling by the dark, dramatic and anguished visions of Tintoretto, who painted the church over a period of more than 20 years.

Virtually every one of Tintoretto's 54 paintings of scenes from both the New and the Old Testaments is a masterpiece, but his intensely moving *Crucifixion* (1565) in the Salla dell'Albergo is arguably the most outstanding. You will find more works by Tintoretto illustrating the life of St Roch in the Renaissance church of San Rocco next door. ⓐ San Polo 3052, Campo San Rocco ⓣ 041 523 4864 ⓦ www.scuolagrandesanrocco.it ⓛ 09.30–17.30 daily (closed Easter) ⓝ Water bus to San Tomà ⓘ Admission charge

RETAIL THERAPY

Aliani Excellent delicatessen and grocery shop. ⓐ San Polo 654, Ruga Vecchia San Giovanni ⓣ 041 522 4913 ⓛ 08.00–13.00, 17.00–19.30 Tues–Sat, closed Sun & Mon ⓝ Water bus to San Silvestro

Emporio il Nido delle Cicogne Stylish children's clothes. ⓐ San Polo 2806, Campo San Tomà ⓣ 041 528 7497 ⓛ 09.30–12.30, 15.30–19.30 Mon–Sat, closed Sun

Gilberto Penzo Handmade models of gondolas and other boats. ⓐ San Polo 2681, Calle Saoneri ⓣ 041 719 372 ⓦ www.veniceboats.com ⓛ 08.30–13.00, 15.00–18.00 Mon–Sat, closed Sun ⓝ Water bus to San Tomà

Hibiscus Colourful jewellery and accessories. ⓐ San Polo 1060, Ruga Rialto ⓣ 041 523 7486 ⓛ 09.30–19.30 Mon–Sat, 11.00–19.30 Sun ⓝ Water bus to San Silvestro

Kirikù Fashionable clothes for kids and women. ❸ San Polo 1463, Calle della Madonetta ❶ 041 296 0619 ❺ 10.00–19.30 Mon–Sat, 11.00–19.00 Sun ❻ Water bus to San Silvestro

Polliero Fine stationery and bookbinding services. ❸ San Polo 2995, Campo dei Frari ❶ 041 528 5130 ❺ 10.00–19.30 Mon–Sat, 10.00–13.00 Sun ❻ Water bus to San Tomà

Tragicomica A dazzling array of masks. ❸ San Polo 2800, Calle dei Nomboli ❶ 041 721 102 ❿ www.tragicomica.it ❺ 10.00–19.00 daily ❻ Water bus to San Tomà

Zazu Chic women's clothing. ❸ San Polo 2750, Calle Saoneri ❶ 041 715 426 ❺ 10.00–14.30, 15.00–19.30 daily ❻ Water bus to San Tomà

TAKING A BREAK

Al Prosecco £ ❶ Wine bar serving good, light meals. ❸ Santa Croce 1503, Campo San Giacomo dell'Orio ❶ 041 524 0222 ❿ www.alprosecco.com ❺ 08.00–20.00 daily; open later in summer ❻ Water bus to San Stae

Al Timon £ ❷ Nautical-themed café with tempting sandwiches, bruschetta and pasta dishes. ❸ San Polo 3057, Campo San Rocco ❶ 041 713 120 ❺ 07.00–20.30 daily ❻ Water bus to San Tomà

Alaska £ ❸ Exciting flavours at this ice-cream parlour. ❸ Santa Croce 1159, Calle Larga dei Bari ❶ 041 715 211 ❺ 11.00–23.00 daily (Apr–Oct); 12.00–21.00 daily (Nov & Jan–Mar); closed Dec ❻ Water bus to Riva di Biasio

Altrove £ ❹ Popular café near the Rialto Bridge. Have a drink, salad or sandwich. ⓐ San Polo 1105, Campo San Silvestro ❶ 041 528 9224 ❺ 08.30–24.00 Mon–Thur, 08.30–01.00 Fri, 09.30–01.00 Sat, closed Sun ❷ Water bus to San Silvestro

Bancogiro £ ❺ Outside tables by the Grand Canal for a glass of wine, some fresh fish from the nearby market or a plate of cheese. ⓐ San Polo 122, Campo San Giacometto ❶ 041 523 2061 ❽ www.osteriabancogiro.it ❺ 12.00–23.00 Tues–Sun, closed Mon ❷ Water bus to Rialto Mercato

● *San Giacometto di Rialto – perhaps Venice's oldest church*

Do Mori £ ❻ Excellent snacks from the counter. ❸ San Polo 429, Calle
dei Do Mori ❶ 041 522 5401 ❻ 08.00–20.30 Mon, Tues & Thur–Sat,
08.00–15.00 Wed, closed Sun ❽ Water bus to Rialto Mercato

Naranzaria £ ❼ Restaurant and bar with outside tables by the
Grand Canal. The Japanese chef serves sushi and impressive salads.
❸ San Polo 130, Erbaria ❶ 041 724 1035 ❾ www.naranzaria.it
❻ Restaurant: 12.00–15.00, 19.30–22.30 daily; bar: 09.30–24.00
Tues–Sun, closed Mon ❽ Water bus to Rialto Mercato

Rizzardini £ ❽ One of the best bakeries around selling snacks
and pastries. ❸ San Polo 1415, Campiello dei Meloni ❶ 041 522 3835
❻ 07.00–20.15 Wed–Mon, closed Tues ❽ Water bus to San Silvestro

Birraria £–££ ❾ Popular bar in an animated square. Go for the pizza or
pasta, or just have a drink. ❸ San Polo 2168, Campo San Polo ❶ 041 275
0570 ❻ 12.00–14.30, 19.00–22.30 daily ❽ Water bus to San Tomà

AFTER DARK

RESTAURANTS

Al Garanghélo £ ❿ Friendly place serving hearty meals in the evening,
with drinks and lighter snacks during the day. ❸ San Polo 1570,
Calle dei Botteri ❶ 041 721 721 ❾ www.algaranghelo.it ❻ 11.00–15.00,
18.00–21.30 Mon–Sat, closed Sun ❽ Water bus to Rialto Mercato

Nono Risorto £ ⓫ Pizzas and Venetian food in this lively place with a
courtyard and a young clientele. ❸ Santa Croce 2338, Sottoportego de
la Siora Bettina ❶ 041 524 1169 ❻ 19.00–22.30 Thur, 12.00–14.30,
19.00–22.30 Fri–Tues, closed Wed ❽ Water bus to San Stae

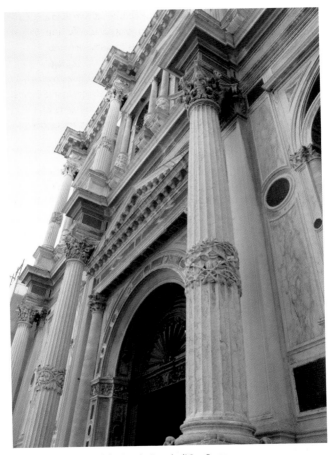

▲ The grand façade of the Scuola Grande di San Rocco

Osteria Mocenigo £–££ ⑫ *Osteria* serving Venetian meals. ⓐ Santa Croce 1919, Salizzada San Stae ① 041 523 1703 ① 12.00–15.00, 19.00–22.30 Tues–Sun, closed Mon ⓝ Water bus to San Stae

Alla Madonna ££ ⑬ Good-value meals and fast service in this packed restaurant near the Rialto Bridge. ⓐ San Polo 594, Calle della Madonna ① 041 522 3824 ⓦ www.ristoranteallamadonna.com ① 12.00–14.30, 19.00–22.00 Thur–Tues, closed Wed ⓝ Water bus to Rialto Mercato

Il Refolo ££ ⑭ Good views from the outside tables of this fashionable but pricey pizzeria. Good selection of other dishes and wines. ⓐ Santa Croce 1459, Campiello del Piovan ① 041 524 0016 ① 19.00–23.00 Tues, 12.00–14.45, 19.00–23.00 Wed–Sun, closed Mon & Nov–Mar ⓝ Water bus to Riva di Biasio

⬥ *Park your gondola right outside your restaurant*

La Zucca ££ ⓯ One of the most popular restaurants in town, this pretty canal-side eatery offers friendly service and a great menu. No fish, but both carnivores and vegetarians are well catered for. ⓐ Santa Croce 1762, Ponte del Megio ⓣ 041 524 1570 ⓦ www.lazucca.it ⓛ 12.00–14.30, 19.00–23.00 Mon–Sat, closed Sun ⓦ Water bus to San Stae

Antiche Carampane ££–£££ ⓰ Excellent fish and seafood in this atmospheric trattoria with an outdoor terrace. Mixed reports about the service. ⓐ San Polo 1911, Calle de la Carampane ⓣ 041 524 0165 ⓦ www.antichecarampane.com ⓛ 12.30–14.30, 19.30–22.30 Tues–Sat, closed Sun & Mon ⓦ Water bus to San Silvestro

Da Fiore £££ ⓱ Upmarket restaurant specialising in fish and seafood, not to be confused with other restaurants using the same name. Art Deco interior and formal service. ⓐ San Polo 2202A, Calle del Scaleter ⓣ 041 721 308 ⓦ www.dafiore.net ⓛ 12.30–14.30, 19.30–22.30 Tues–Sat, closed Sun & Mon ⓦ Water bus to San Tomà

BARS
Ai Postali Outside tables and snacks in this popular late-opening bar near the railway station. ⓐ Santa Croce 821, Fondamenta Rio Marin ⓣ 041 715 156 ⓛ 19.30–02.00 Mon–Sat, closed Sun & two wks Aug ⓦ Water bus to Riva di Biasio

Da Baffo A lively, late-opening bar with a great selection of traditional snacks. ⓐ San Polo 2346, Campo Sant'Agostino ⓣ 041 520 8862 ⓛ 07.30–02.00 Mon–Sat, 10.00–24.00 Sun ⓦ Water bus to San Tomà

Cannaregio

The district of Cannaregio, once Venice's main manufacturing area, is spacious and pleasant with broad canal sides and a fairly simple layout. Shops, bars and hotels tend to be cheaper and the area is more popular with locals than the city centre. The backstreets here in Cannaregio, where over a third of the city's population live, are where you will find the 'real' people in Venice.

The Strada Nova is a broad, hectic street running along the Grand Canal, leading from the Rialto Bridge to the Ca' d'Oro museum and packed with shops and cafés as well as tourists. Equally bustling is the Lista di Spagna near the railway station, full of touristy cafés and shops. To see a bit more of the 'real' Venice you have to venture away from these streets.

The Fondamenta della Sensa and the parallel Fondamenta della Misericordia both offer peaceful walks. Look out for the plaque marking Tintoretto's former house at No 3399 Fondamenta dei Mori, near the bridge by the Campo dei Mori. From the quayside of Fondamente Nuove you can get fine views of the lagoon, the cemetery island of San Michele and, beyond it, Murano.

SIGHTS & ATTRACTIONS

Gesuiti (Santa Maria Assunta)

Not to be confused with the Gesuati in Dorsoduro, this 18th-century Baroque church is the first of those built by the Jesuits in the city. Both the exterior and interior are strikingly ornate, some say to the point of vulgarity. Titian's *Martyrdom of St Lawrence* (1558) is above the altar on the left. ⓐ Campo dei Gesuiti ⓣ 041 528 6579 ⓛ 10.00–12.00, 16.00–18.00 daily ⓦ Water bus to Fondamente Nuove

Madonna dell'Orto (Madonna of the Orchard)

This pleasant church in a small square has an attractive red brick façade displaying a marble sculpture of St Christopher, to whom it was originally dedicated. The church was founded in the 14th century and modified in the 15th, making the façade a mixture of Romanesque, Gothic and Renaissance styles. Inside, it is pleasantly peaceful, light and uncluttered. You will find several superb works by Tintoretto, who lived nearby and is buried here in a small chapel off the

◔ *Inside the lovely Madonna dell'Orto are works by Tintoretto*

right-hand aisle. ⊙ Campo della Madonna dell'Orto ⊙ 041 275 0642
ⓦ www.chorusvenezia.org ⊙ 10.00–17.00 Mon–Sat, closed Sun
ⓝ Water bus to Madonna dell'Orto ① Admission charge

THE JEWISH GHETTO

One of the most interesting areas is the Ghetto, east of the station and north of the Strada Nuova, in which Jews were at one time confined. A *geto*, or 'foundry', once occupied the area and this gave its name to other ghettos round the world.

The ghetto was closed off by gates so that between 1516 and the end of the 18th century Jews were allowed out only during the day and only then if they wore identifiable clothing. As their numbers grew, they could only build upwards. Napoleon removed the gates in 1797 but the Austrians who subsequently occupied Venice confined the Jews again until the end of their rule in 1866.

Although few Jews live there now, there are still a number of Jewish shops and synagogues in the area. You can also see a monument to Holocaust victims transported from Venice (on a wall in the main square) and visit the small **Museo Ebraico** (Jewish Museum ⊙ Cannaregio 2902B, Campo del Ghetto Nuovo ⊙ 041 715 359 ⓦ www.museoebraico.it ⊙ 10.00–19.00 Sun–Fri, closed Sat (June–Sept); 10.00–18.00 Sun–Fri, closed Sat (Oct–May) ⓝ Water bus to San Marcuola or Guglie). Guided tours in English of the beautiful hidden synagogues are available at the museum. Near the Ghetto is the lively **Rio Terrà San Leonardo** street market (⊙ 08.00–12.30 Mon–Sat ⓝ Water bus to San Marcuola or Guglie).

Santa Maria dei Miracoli (St Mary of the Miracles)

Popular for local weddings, this church is arguably one of the most beautiful in Venice for its colourful, luminous marble façade. Go early in the morning or late afternoon when the sun falls on its best features. Exquisitely designed in Renaissance style by Pietro Lombardo, it was built in 1481–9 to house an image of the Virgin by Niccolò di Pietro, which was thought to be responsible for a number of miracles. The image is now on display above the high altar.

The interior contains some fine sculptures and also uses coloured marble. Note the 16th-century barrel-vaulted ceiling with its portraits of saints. ❸ Cannaregio 6075, Campiello dei Miracoli ❶ 041 275 0462 Ⓦ www.chorusvenezia.org 🕙 10.00–17.00 Mon–Sat, closed Sun Ⓝ Water bus to Ca' d'Oro ❶ Admission charge

CULTURE

Ca' d'Oro (House of Gold)

The façade of the 'House of Gold' is one of the most impressive, and best known, of any palazzo on the Grand Canal. The building is arguably the prime example of Byzantine-influenced 15th-century Gothic architecture in the city. Built by the aristocratic merchant Marino Contarini in 1420, its exterior was designed to be the most luxurious in Venice, originally featuring gold leaf. After Contarini's death, the subsequent series of owners altered the building substantially, sometimes disastrously. It was restored to its former splendour by Baron Franchetti and left to the state in 1916.

Franchetti's own collection of art, furniture and tapestries is housed in a museum spread over two floors. The highlight is Andrea Mantegna's celebrated *St Sebastian* (1506). Also look out for Carpaccio's early 16th-century *Annunciation and Death of the Virgin*.

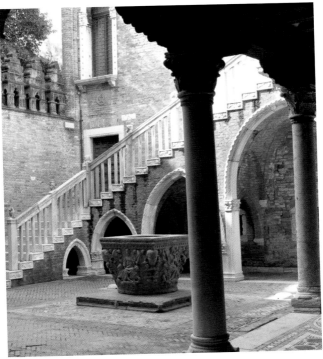

● *The Ca' d'Oro should not be missed*

The entrance is in a small alleyway off the Strada Nuova and there are excellent views from both floors. ⓐ Cannaregio 3932, Calle della Ca' d'Oro ⓒ 041 520 0345 ⓦ www.cadoro.org ⓒ 08.15–14.00 Mon, 08.15–19.15 Tues–Sat, closed Sun; last entry 30 mins before closing ⓝ Water bus to Ca' d'Oro ⓘ Admission charge

RETAIL THERAPY

Do Maghi Colourful glass vases and other objects with modern designs. ⓐ Cannaregio 2328 ⓣ 041 524 4719 ⓦ www.domaghi.com ⓛ 10.00–19.30 Mon–Sat, 10.30–19.00 Sun ⓝ Water bus to Rialto

Gian Paolo Tolotti One of Venice's leading antique shops. ⓐ Calle del Forno 42 ⓣ 041 528 5262 ⓛ 09.00–12.00, 16.00–19.00 Mon–Sat, closed Sun ⓝ Water bus to Ca' d'Oro

Laboratorio Blu Children's bookshop with a good selection of English-language books. ⓐ Cannaregio 1224, Campo del Ghetto Vecchio ⓣ 041 715 819 ⓛ 16.00–19.30 Mon, 09.30–12.30, 16.00–19.30 Tues–Sat, closed Sun ⓝ Water bus to San Marcuola

🔺 *Strada Nuova is the main shopping street in Venice*

Mori & Bozzi Fashionable shoe shop. ⓐ Cannaregio 2367, Rio Terra Maddalena ⓣ 041 715 261 ⓛ 09.30–12.30, 15.30–19.30 Mon–Sat, 11.00–19.00 Sun ⓦ Water bus to San Marcuola

Vittorio Costantini Glass-blower and designer selling intricate glass animals and birds. ⓐ Cannaregio 5311, Calle del Fumo ⓣ 041 522 2265 ⓦ www.popweb.com/costantini ⓛ 09.15–13.00, 14.15–17.30 Mon–Fri, closed Sat & Sun ⓦ Water bus to Fondamente Nuove

TAKING A BREAK

Boscolo £ ❶ Drinks, pizzas or sweet treats from this bakery. ⓐ Cannaregio 1818, Campiello de l'Anconeta ⓣ 041 720 731 ⓛ 07.00–20.00 daily ⓦ Water bus to San Marcuola

Canottieri £ ❷ Popular with students for its good-value light lunches or fuller evening meals. Good range of fish. ⓐ Cannaregio 690, Fondamenta di San Giobbe ⓣ 041 717 999 ⓛ 08.00–15.00, 19.00–23.00 Tues–Fri, 19.00–23.00 Sat, closed Sun & Mon (Easter–Sept); 08.00–15.00, 19.00–23.00 Tues–Sat, closed Sun & Mon (Oct–Easter) ⓦ Water bus to Crea or Tre Archi ⓘ Hours may vary

La Cantina £ ❸ Buzzing, popular bar with excellent snacks. ⓐ Cannaregio 3689, Campo San Felice ⓣ 041 522 8258 ⓛ 11.00–22.00 Mon–Sat, closed Sun ⓦ Water bus to Ca' d'Oro

Cea £ ❹ Good for pasta, salad or simply an outdoor drink. ⓐ Cannaregio 5422A, Campiello Stella ⓣ 041 523 7450 ⓛ 09.00–14.30, 17.00–21.00 Mon–Fri, 09.00–14.30 Sat, closed Sun ⓦ Water bus to Fondamente Nuove

Da Alberto £ ❺ Good hot and cold food in a comforting environment. ❷ Cannaregio 5401, Calle Larga Giacinto Gallina ❶ 041 523 8153 ❷ 10.30–15.00, 18.30–22.00 Mon–Sat, closed Sun ❷ Water bus to Ospedale

Do Colonne £ ❻ Good range of snacks and sandwiches and a few hot meals. ❷ Cannaregio 1814C, Rio Terrà San Leonardo ❶ 041 524 0453 ❷ 10.00–20.30 Sun–Fri, closed Sat ❷ Water bus to San Marcuola

Il Gelatone £ ❼ Rich ice cream in an interesting range of flavours. ❷ Cannaregio 2063, Rio Terra della Maddalena ❶ 041 720 631 ❷ 10.30–23.00 daily (May–Sept); 10.30–20.30 daily (Oct); closed Nov–Apr ❷ Water bus to San Marcuola

Algiubagiò £–££ ❽ Inspiring views of the lagoon from the terrace. ❷ Cannaregio 5039, Fondamente Nuove ❶ 041 523 6084 ❿ www.algiubagio.net ❷ 07.30–24.00 Wed–Mon, closed Tues ❷ Water bus to Fondamente Nuove

Anice Stellato £–££ ❾ Venetian specialities. ❷ Cannaregio 3272, Fondamenta della Sensa ❶ 041 720 744 ❷ 12.30–14.00, 19.30–22.00 Wed–Sun, closed Mon & Tues ❷ Water bus to Ca' d'Oro

AFTER DARK

RESTAURANTS
Ai Quattro Rusteghi £ ❿ Friendly staff and outdoor seating make this a pleasurable place to spend an evening. ❷ Cannaregio 2888, Campo del Ghetto Nuovo ❶ 041 715 160 ❷ 12.00–14.30, 19.00–23.00 daily ❷ Water bus to San Marcuola or Guglie

Alla Frasca £ ⓫ Pretty *osteria* with southern Italian food and good home-made pasta. ❷ Cannaregio 5176, Campiello della Carità ❶ 041 528 5433 ❷ 11.00–15.00, 18.30–23.00 Tues–Sun, closed Mon Ⓦ Water bus to Fondamente Nuove

Dalla Marisa £–££ ⓬ Rich meat and game dishes in this tiny restaurant with canal-side tables. Booking recommended. ❷ Cannaregio 625B, Fondamenta di San Giobbe ❶ 041 720 211 ❷ 12.00–14.30 Mon, Wed & Sun, 12.00–14.30, 20.00–21.15 Tues & Thur–Sat Ⓦ Water bus to Crea

Bea Vita ££ ⓭ Traditional food with a modern twist. ❷ Cannaregio 3082, Fondamenta delle Cappuccine ❶ 041 275 9347 ❷ 12.00–14.00, 19.15–22.00 Mon–Sat, closed Sun Ⓦ Water bus to Sant'Alvise

Boccadoro ££ ⓮ Worth seeking out for its great fresh fish and seafood. Outside tables. ❷ Cannaregio 5405A, Campiello Widmann ❶ 041 521 1021 Ⓦ www.boccadorovenezia.it ❷ 12.30–14.30, 19.30–22.30 Tues–Sun, closed Mon Ⓦ Water bus to Rialto

Ca' d'Oro (Alla Vedova) ££ ⓯ A long-standing favourite with locals, good for a snack during the day or a traditional Venetian meal in the evening. ❷ Cannaregio 3912, Ramo Ca' d'Oro ❶ 041 528 5524 ❷ 11.30–14.30, 18.30–23.30 Mon–Wed, Fri & Sat, 18.30–23.30 Sun, closed Thur Ⓦ Water bus to Ca' d'Oro

Da Rioba ££ ⓰ Bare bricks and beams create a cosy atmosphere, with outdoor seating in summer. Seafood dishes with a twist. ❷ Cannaregio 2553, Fondamenta della Misericordia ❶ 041 524 4379 Ⓦ www.rioba.it ❷ 12.00–14.30, 19.30–22.30 Tues–Sun; closed Mon & three wks Jan Ⓦ Water bus to Tre Archi or Ca' d'Oro

Fiaschetteria Toscana ££ **⑰** Fine Venetian-style food in a pleasant atmosphere. Excellent desserts. **ⓐ** Cannaregio 5719, Salizada San Giovanni Crisostomo **ⓣ** 041 528 5281 **ⓦ** www.fiaschetteriatoscana.it **ⓛ** 12.30–14.30, 19.30–22.30 Thur–Mon, 19.30–22.30 Wed, closed Tues **ⓝ** Water bus to Rialto

⬥ *A beautiful, traditional canal house*

Vini da Gigio ££ ⑱ Good food and extensive wine list in this romantic but busy restaurant. ⓐ Cannaregio 3628A, Fondamenta della Chiesa ⓣ 041 528 5140 ⓦ www.vinidagigio.com ⓛ 12.00–14.30, 19.30–22.30 Wed–Sun, closed Mon & Tues ⓝ Water bus to Ca' d'Oro

BARS

Al Parlamento Bar with disco music some evenings attracting a young crowd. Sandwiches and snacks available. ⓐ Cannaregio 511, Fondamenta di San Giobbe ⓣ 041 244 0214 ⓛ 08.00–02.00 daily ⓝ Water bus to Crea

Irish Pub A popular Irish pub near Strada Nuova. ⓐ Cannaregio 3847, Corte dei Pali Già Testori ⓣ 041 523 9930 ⓛ 17.00–01.00 daily ⓝ Water bus to Ca' d'Oro

Mondo di Vino Superb wines and snacks. ⓐ Cannaregio 5984A, Salizada San Canciano ⓣ 041 521 1093 ⓛ 10.00–15.00, 17.30–22.00 daily ⓝ Water bus to Rialto

Paradiso Perduto Well-known and popular bar with restaurant, open late with music and sometimes poetry in the evenings. ⓐ Cannaregio 2540, Fondamenta della Misericordia ⓣ 041 720 581 ⓛ 19.00–02.00 Mon & Thur, 12.00–02.00 Fri–Sun, closed Tues & Wed ⓝ Water bus to San Marcuola

Santo Bevitore Friendly pub with a selection of real ales, reasonably priced snacks and live jazz on Mondays. ⓐ Cannaregio 2393A, Fondamenta Diedo, Campo Santa Fosca ⓣ 041 717 560 ⓛ 07.00–24.00 Mon–Fri, 09.30–01.30 Sat, closed Sun ⓝ Water bus to San Marcuola

CASINO CHIC

Venice's smart casino is housed in an early 16th-century Renaissance building on the Grand Canal. A plaque outside commemorates the death of Wagner in the building in 1883. Photo ID and smart dress, including jacket and tie for men, are required. ➌ Cannaregio 2040, Palazzo Vendramin Calergi, Calle Larga Vendramin (off Rio Terra del Maddalena) ➊ 041 529 7111 Ⓦ www.casinovenezia.it ⌚ 15.30–02.30 Mon–Thur, 15.30–03.00 Fri & Sat, closed Sun Ⓦ Water bus to San Marcuola ❶ Admission charge

THEATRE

Teatro Fondamenta Nuove Theatre mainly hosting performances of contemporary dance. ➌ Cannaregio 5013, Fondamente Nuove ➊ 041 522 4498 Ⓦ www.teatrofondamentanuove.it Ⓦ Water bus to Fondamente Nuove

Teatro Malibran Originally built in 1678; performances of opera, ballet and classical music. ➌ Cannaregio 5873, Campiello Malibran ➊ 041 786 511/041 2424 (call centre) Ⓦ www.teatrolafenice.it Ⓦ Water bus to Rialto

◗ *San Donato Basilica in Murano*

OUT OF TOWN
trips

The Lido, Giudecca & San Giorgio Maggiore

The islands of the southern lagoon are just a short trip from the city centre by water bus and are well worth a day trip for their change of atmosphere. There are superb views of Venice from both Giudecca and San Giorgio.

GETTING THERE

You can take water bus Nos 1, 2, 51 or 52 straight to the Lido. No 1 leaves from all stops along the Grand Canal, and Nos 51 and 52 depart from the San Zaccaria stop, just along from the Palazzo Ducale. It takes no more than 15 minutes from San Zaccaria.

To reach San Giorgio and Giudecca, take water bus No 2 from anywhere along the Grand Canal or from the San Zaccaria or Zattere stops.

SIGHTS & ATTRACTIONS

THE LIDO

The Lido is Venice's beach resort, a fashionable holiday destination since the early 20th century when the luxurious Excelsior and Des Bains hotels first opened. It is basically a 12-km (7^1/$_2$-mile) sandbank with long, straight roads and broad, shaded avenues. The main street is Gran Viale Santa Maria Elisabetta, where many hotels, restaurants and shops can be found. The Lido is also a residential suburb; cars are allowed and, in contrast to Venice, the houses and villas here are modern in design and many are decorated in Art Nouveau or Art Deco styles. The Lido is the place to get away from frantic sightseeing – take the time to relax and enjoy the atmosphere.

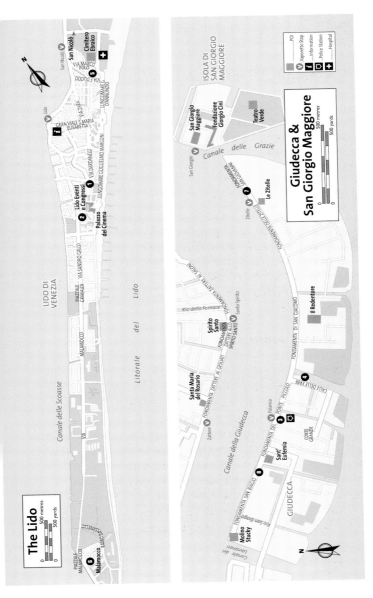

The Lido

0 — 500 metres
0 — 500 yards

LIDO DI VENEZIA

Canale delle Scoasse

Litorale del Lido

San Nicolò

Cimitero Ebraico

VIA MARCO POLO
LUNGOMARE D'ANNUNZIO
VIA DUODO

Lido

GRAN VIALE S MARIA ELISABETTA

VIA TARA

VIA DARDANELLI

LUNGOMARE GUGLIELMO MARCONI

Lido Eventi e Congressi

Palazzo del Cinema

PIAZZALE GRIMALDI

VIA SANDRO GALLO

VIA

PIAZZALE MALAMOCCO

Malamocco

N

Giudecca & San Giorgio Maggiore

0 — 500 metres
0 — 500 yards

ISOLA DI SAN GIORGIO MAGGIORE

San Giorgio Maggiore

Fondazione Giorgio Cini

Teatro Verde

Canale delle Grazie

San Giorgio

FONDAMENTA ZITELLE

Le Zitelle

Zitelle

FONDAMENTA SANT'EUFEMIA

FONDAMENTA DELLE ZITELLE

Il Redentore

FONDAMENTA DI SAN GIACOMO

CALLE DELLE ERBE

CORTE GRANDE

Palanca

FONDAMENTA DEL PONTE PICCOLO

Sant' Eufemia

Canale della Giudecca

GIUDECCA

FONDAMENTA SAN BIAGIO

Rio San Biagio

Canale dei Lavoranti

Molino Stucky

Santa Maria del Rosario

Rio della Fornace

FONDAMENTA ZATTERE AL PONTE LUNGO

FONDAMENTA ZATTERE AI GESUATI

Zattere

Spirito Santo

FONDAMENTA ZATTERE ALLO SPIRITO SANTO

FONDAMENTA ZATTERE AI SALONI

Santo Spirito

N

POI
Vaporetto Stop
Information
Police Station
Hospital

Beach

The sandbank stretches along most of the southern side of the island, with occasional private areas reserved for hotel guests. In most areas there are huts and umbrellas for hire, but these areas charge an entrance fee. The Blue Moon beach at the end of the Gran Viale is free and the Alberoni and San Nicolò beaches are usually the quietest. The beach is a 15-minute walk from the Gran Viale Santa Maria Elisabetta water bus stop, which is also the departure point for taxis and various regular road bus routes to all parts of the Lido.

VENICE INTERNATIONAL FILM FESTIVAL

The Lido heaves in late August and early September with cinema lovers flocking for the annual Film Festival. The event is attended by top international film producers and actors hoping for the *Leone D'Oro* (Golden Lion) award and is a showcase for both mainstream and art-house films. The area around the multi-screen Palazzo del Cinema and the old Casino buzzes with activity and film stars can be spotted hanging out at the luxurious Excelsior Hotel. The festival actually started at the Excelsior in 1932 – the first cinema event of its kind in the world – and was so successful that the Palazzo del Cinema was built four years later to host it.

You can get season tickets or tickets for individual films, but do book well in advance.

Mostra Internazionale D'Arte Cinematografica
ⓐ Palazzo del Cinema, Lungomare Marconi 90
ⓣ 041 521 8711 ⓦ www.labiennale.org

Malamocco

The village of Malamocco at the western end of the island is a good place to enjoy a lazy meal of excellent fish and seafood. Ⓥ Bus: B

San Nicolò

At the eastern end of the Lido is the San Nicolò area, which has a 15th-century fortress as well as the 11th-century church which forms the main focus of the festival of La Sensa (see page 9). There is also the **Cimitero Ebraico**, a Jewish cemetery dating from 1386 (Ⓐ Via Cipro ❶ 041 715 359 ❶ 041 72 3007 Ⓔ prenotazioni@codesscultura.it), but you must book in advance to visit Ⓥ Bus: A

Sport

Opportunities for sport and exercise are much better on the Lido than in Venice itself. You can hire a bicycle from **Lido On Bike** (Ⓐ Gran Viale 21B ❶ 041 526 8019 Ⓦ www.lidoonbike.it) or **Giorgio Barberi** (Ⓐ Via Zara 5 ❶ 041 526 14 90), play golf at the **Circolo Golf Venezia** (Ⓐ Strada Vecchia 1 ❶ 041 731 333 Ⓦ www.circologolfvenezia.it), enjoy tennis at the **Tennis Club Ca' del Moro** (Ⓐ Via Ferruccio Parri 6 ❶ 041 770 965 Ⓦ www.tennisclubcadelmoro.it) or go for a swim at the public pool **Piscina Ca' Bianca** (Ⓐ Via Sandro Gallo, Lido ❶ 041 526 2222).

GIUDECCA

Originally filled with palazzos and pleasure gardens, by the 19th century Giudecca had become a site for factories, prisons and warehouses. Reinvented yet again in the 20th century, it is today a pleasant residential suburb of Venice well-known for its luxurious Cipriani hotel (see page 37). Elton John has a property on the island. When you reach Giudecca, look back over Venice from the quayside. The southern end also has some wonderful views of the lagoon.

Giudecca is tiny and it is quick and easy to walk to all destinations. If you do need to use public transport, there are three water-bus stops: Zitelle, Redentore and Palanca.

Il Redentore (The Redeemer)

Palladio's magnificent domed Church of the Redeemer was built in 1592 to give thanks for the end of a plague which killed 50,000 Venetians. During the colourful **Festa del Redentore** in late July (see page 10), a pontoon bridge is laid across the Giudecca Canal from Zattere to the church.

The façade is in the style of a grand classical temple but the interior is fairly modest, containing paintings by Vivarini and Veronese. ⓐ Giudecca 195, Campo del Redentore ❶ 041 275 0462 ⓦ www.chorusvenezia.org ❶ 10.00–17.00 Mon–Sat, closed Sun ⓝ Water bus to Redentore ❶ Admission charge

SAN GIORGIO MAGGIORE

This tiny island, just across the lagoon from St Mark's Square, is worth a visit for its landmark church of the same name and its Benedictine monastery of Fondazione Giorgio Cini.

Fondazione Giorgio Cini

This late 10th-century Benedictine monastery once enjoyed considerable wealth and prestige, welcoming powerful visitors such as Florentine Cosimo de' Medici, who commissioned a great library for it in the 15th century.

The monastery was enlarged in the 16th century with a fine refectory and cloisters designed by Andrea Palladio. Its fortunes changed, however, when Napoleon took over and the building became an artillery headquarters.

◔ *Il Redentore at sunset*

● *San Giorgio Maggiore was part of the old Benedictine monastery*

It was not until 1951 that it was bought by Count Vittorio Cini, carefully restored and turned into an international cultural centre. It has since hosted major international conferences including the G7 summits of 1980 and 1987. Temporary art exhibitions and concerts complement the permanent collection of works by Tintoretto. Visit is by guided tour only, with regular English-language tours lasting approximately one hour. Check the website for details. ❸ Isola di San Giorgio ☎ 041 271 0229 Ⓦ www.cini.it ⏰ Guided tours every 30 mins at 10.00–17.00 Sat & Sun (May–Sept); 10.00–16.00 Sat & Sun (Oct–Apr) 🚤 Water bus to San Giorgio ❶ Admission charge

San Giorgio Maggiore

Andrea Palladio's distinctive style of architecture is clearly visible in the capacious, harmonious and beautifully proportioned interior of this church. Tintoretto's *Last Supper* and *Manna from Heaven* are here as well as works by Carpaccio and Palma il Giovane.

Take the lift up the bell tower for some wonderful views. ⓐ Isola di San Giorgio ① 041 522 7827 ⓛ 09.30–12.30, 14.30–18.00 daily (May–Sept); 09.30–12.30, 14.30–17.00 daily (Oct–Apr) ⓝ Water bus to San Giorgio ① Admission charge for bell tower

RETAIL THERAPY

There are several Italian chain stores along the Gran Viale, but in general it is best to take a break from shopping when visiting the islands. For a modestly priced department store with a supermarket, try **Oviesse** ⓐ Via Corfu 1, Lido ① 041 526 5720 ⓛ 09.00–20.00 Mon–Sat, 09.00–13.00, 15.30–19.30 Sun ⓝ Water bus to Lido

TAKING A BREAK & AFTER DARK

Pasticceria Maggion £ ❶ Excellent pastries. ⓐ Via Dardanelli 46A, Lido ① 041 526 0836 ⓝ Water bus to Lido

Trento £ ❷ This popular bar serves simple but tasty food. ⓐ Via Sandro Gallo 82E, Lido ① 041 526 5960 ⓛ 07.00–21.00 daily (Apr–Sept); 07.00–21.00 Mon–Sat, closed Sun (Oct–Mar) ⓝ Water bus to Lido

Alla Palanca £–££ ❸ A friendly welcome, and a great view. ⓐ Giudecca 448, Fondamenta del Ponte Piccolo ① 041 528 7719 ⓛ 07.00–20.30 Mon–Sat, closed Sun ⓝ Water bus to Palanca

Altanella ££ ❹ Fish restaurant with a pleasant terrace.
ⓐ Giudecca 268, Calle delle Erbe ❶ 041 522 7780 ❶ 12.30–14.00,
19.30–21.00 Wed–Sun, closed Mon & Tues ❻ Water bus to Palanca

La Favorita ££ ❺ Traditional Venetian dishes in a calm atmosphere.
ⓐ Via Francesca Duodo 33, Lido ❶ 041 526 1626 ❶ 19.30–22.30 Tues,
12.30–14.30, 19.30–22.30 Wed–Sun, closed Mon ❻ Water bus to Lido

Trattoria Scarso ££ ❻ A simple, traditional fish restaurant in
the village of Malamocco. ⓐ Piazzale Malamocco 5, Lido ❶ 041 770
834 ❶ 11.00–15.00, 19.00–21.30 Wed–Mon, closed Tues (Mar–Oct);
11.00–15.00 Wed–Mon, closed Tues (Dec–Feb) ❻ Water bus to Lido

Cip's Club ££–£££ ❼ One of the restaurants at the Cipriani hotel;
superb views of Venice from the terrace. ⓐ Giudecca 10, Fondamenta
delle Zitelle ❶ 041 520 7744 ❿ www.cipriani.com ❶ 19.30–23.00 daily
(Apr–Oct); closed Nov–Mar ❻ Water bus to Zitelle

▲ Enjoy a meal with a view at Cip's Club

Harry's Dolci ££–£££ ❽ An offshoot of the renowned Harry's Bar, with great views from the terrace. ❸ Giudecca 773, Fondamenta San Biagio ❶ 041 522 4844 ❿ www.cipriani.com ❺ 10.30–23.00 Mon eve–Sun (drinks and snacks); 12.00–15.00, 19.00–22.30 Mon eve–Sun (full meals) (Apr–Oct); closed Nov–Mar ⓝ Water bus to Palanca

ACCOMMODATION

Ostello Venezia £ This cheap and cheerful hostel provides clean dorms and family rooms, some of them with private bathrooms. Its location means it is a peaceful haven, while offering great views of the city. St Mark's is just a five-minute boat ride away. ❸ Fondamenta delle Zitelle 86 ❶ 041 523 8211 ❿ www.hostelvenice.org ⓝ Water bus to Zitelle

Belvedere ££ Long-established hotel near the main water-bus stop. ❸ Piazzale Santa Maria Elisabetta 4, Lido ❶ 041 526 0115 ❿ www.belvedere-venezia.com ⓝ Water bus to Lido

Villa Cipro ££ Pleasantly decorated rooms and a pretty courtyard. ❸ Via Zara 2, Lido ❶ 041 731 538 ❿ www.hotelvillacipro.com ❺ Mar–Dec; closed Jan & Feb ⓝ Water bus to Lido

Bauer Palladio Hotel £££ Charming hotel and spa overlooking St Mark's Basin. ❸ Giudecca 33 ❶ 041 270 3806 ❿ www.bauerhotels.com ❺ Apr–Oct; closed Nov–Mar ⓝ Water bus to Palanca

Excelsior £££ This luxurious Moorish palazzo boasts all creature comforts plus a pool and private beach. ❸ Lungomare Marconi 41, Lido ❶ 041 526 0201 ❿ www.starwood.com ❺ May–Oct; closed Nov–Mar ⓝ Water bus to Lido; regular boat shuttle to Venice for hotel guests

Murano, Torcello & Burano

The ancient lagoon islands of Murano, Torcello and Burano are worth visiting not only to escape from the bustle of Venice but also for the enjoyable trip across the lagoon.

GETTING THERE

Water buses Nos 41 and 42 from Fondamente Nuove will take you straight to nearby Murano. For Torcello and Burano take the Linea LN (Laguna Nord) water bus from either San Zaccaria or Fondamente Nuove.

SIGHTS & ATTRACTIONS

MURANO
Museo del Vetro (Glass Museum)

Exhibits ranging from ancient Roman glass to modern Murano designs are arranged chronologically in this 17th-century palazzo, once home to the bishops of Torcello. It is a great place to get a perspective on the rich history of glass-making behind the island's thriving industry. ⊙ Fondamenta Giustinian 8 ☎ 041 739 586 ⓦ www.museicivicieneziani.it 🕓 10.00–18.00 Thur–Tues, closed Wed (Apr–Oct); 10.00–17.00 Thur–Tues, closed Wed (Nov–Mar); last entry 30 mins before closing 🚤 Water bus to Museo

Santi Maria e Donato

This serene basilica is thought to have been founded as early as the 7th century. The main façade is clearly Byzantine influenced with a colonnaded apse, while the interior has five Greek marble columns

Murano

Cimitero

C.P. VENINI

FOND. CRISTOFORO PARMENSE

Canale di Tessera

Canale Serenella

Canale Ondello

SACCA SERENELLA

Serenella

C. DIETRO GLI ORTI

C. S COPRIANO

C. BERTOLINI

FOND. DEI VETRAI

FOND. G. MANIN

CALLE MIOTTI

FOND. SERENELLA

Colonna

Santa Maria degli Angeli

FOND. SEBASTIANO VENIER

CALLE BERNARDO

CAMPO S SALVADOR

CAMPO S BERNARDO

FOND. SANTI

CALLE CONTERIE

COL CONVENTO

CALLE VOLPI

FOND. DA L RADI

CIVRARIN

Palazzo da Mula

FOND. COLLEONI

S Pietro Martire

CAMPO S STEFANO

MURANO

FOND. GIOVANNI DEI BATTUTI

Museo del Vetro

Museo

FOND. DA MULA

FOND. MARCO GIUSTINIAN

S Maria e Donato

Palazzo Trevisan

Navagero

Faro

Canale dei Marani

N

0   100 metres
0   100 yards

Torcello & Burano

0   250 metres
0   250 yards

N

Canale dei Borgognoni

Canale Sant'Antonio

TORCELLO

Museo Estuario

Santa Maria Assunta & Campanile

PIAZZA TORCELLO

FOND. BORGOGNONI

Ponte del Diavolo

② V Torcello

Mazzorbo

FONDAMENTA DI SANTA CATERINA

MAZZORBO

③

RADA DEL CIMITERO

STRADA DI CORTE COMARE

STRADA S MAURO

Burano V

FOND. DELLA GIUDECCA

FOND. CAVANELLA

CORTE COMARE

CAMPO VIGNER

FONDAMENTA PESCHERIA

PIAZZA GALUPPI

VIA BALDASSARE GALUPPI

VIA DI VIGNA

VIA PONTINELLO D'ESTRA

FOND. MANDRACCHIO

FONDAMENTA TERRANOVA

FONDAMENTA CAO MOLECA

BURANO

Museo del Merletto

④ **Chiesa di San Martino**

①

■ POI

V Vaporetto Stop

○ *Visit Murano for its fascinating glass museum*

down each side. The 12th-century floor and the apse both feature mosaics and the square bell tower is also characteristic of the 12th- and 13th-century Veneto-Byzantine style. The church was restored in the 19th century and retains its original beauty despite missing the top of its steeple. ❸ Campo San Donato ❶ 041 739 056 ◐ 08.30–18.00 daily ◍ Water bus to Museo

TORCELLO

Venetians started flocking to Torcello in the 5th and 6th centuries to escape invading tribes. The island had a population of 20,000 by the 14th century and was filled with fine palazzos and churches. The marshy land made the area unhealthy, however, and by the 15th century many of its inhabitants escaped the danger of malaria by moving to Venice, which was prospering at the time. Today only a handful of people live here but it is a refreshing contrast to Venice, with a few restaurants and the odd souvenir stall.

Campanile (Bell Tower)

A climb to the top of the basilica's bell tower will give you magnificent views of the lagoon. ❸ Santa Maria Assunta 🕐 10.30–17.30 daily (Mar–Oct); 10.30–16.30 daily (Nov–Feb); last entry 30 mins before closing 🚤 Water bus to Torcello ❶ Admission charge

Santa Maria Assunta

The oldest building in the lagoon, this Veneto-Byzantine-style basilica dates from as early as 639. Most of what you see today, however, was built in the early 11th century. Look closely at the intricate mosaics on both the floor and walls, in particular the *Madonna and Child* in the central apse, and at the marble choir screen. ❸ Torcello ❶ 041 296 0630 🕐 10.30–18.00 daily (Mar–Oct); 10.00–17.00 daily (Nov–Feb); last entry 30 mins before closing 🚤 Water bus to Torcello ❶ Admission charge

ISLAND TOURS

Another good way of seeing the islands is to take an organised tour. **Alilaguna** (🕐 041 241 1711 🌐 alilaguna.com) runs good-value multilingual group tours of the islands, leaving twice a day in summer and once daily in winter, with tours lasting around four hours. For a private tour in English or another language, contact the **Cooperativa Guide Turistiche** (❸ San Marco 750, Calle Morosini de la Regina ❶ 041 520 9038 🌐 www.guidevenezia.it 🕐 09.00–13.00, 14.00–18.00 Mon–Fri, 09.00–13.00 Sat, closed Sun (June–Aug); 09.00–17.00 Mon–Fri, 09.00–13.00 Sat, closed Sun (Sept–May) 🚤 Water bus to San Zaccaria) ❶ Advance booking is advisable

● *Burano has a rather different style to Venice*

BURANO

The vividly coloured houses on the island of Burano make it one of the most picturesque places in the lagoon. It is famous for its lacemaking and also has a thriving fishing industry. With a population of just 5,000, it is a quiet and pleasant place to stroll around admiring the intricate lace on sale and seeing the fishermen land their catch, repair their nets or paint their boats.

When you are tired of wandering around, stop for a drink near the church of San Martino with its tilting bell tower or choose a restaurant to enjoy some excellent fresh fish.

RETAIL THERAPY

The only things worth buying – but they really are worth buying – are glass and lace on the islands that make them.

MURANO

Barovier & Toso Well-established glass-maker producing impressive contemporary designs. ⓐ Fondamenta dei Vetrai 28 ☎ 041 739 049 ⓦ www.barovier.com ⏱ 10.00–12.30, 13.00–17.00 Mon–Fri, closed Sat & Sun ⓦ Water bus to Colonna

MURANO GLASS

Glass-makers began moving from Venice to Murano in the late 13th century. The industry made the island – which is actually nine small islands linked by bridges – prosperous and it once had a population of 30,000. Although only 5,000 people live there today, the industry continues to thrive and Murano glass is exported around the world.

For a unique experience, visit the glass-blowing factories and workshops, where many the glass-blowers will demonstrate their craft for you. There will be plenty of locals on the quayside when you arrive offering to take you to the workshops. By all means go along, but don't feel obliged to tip them or to part with your money before taking a good look round.

Whatever you buy, do check that it is authentic Murano glass and not an inferior, imported product. Look for the Vetro Artistico trademark and be prepared to pay a high price in return for quality. The Retail Therapy section lists several established quality glass shops.

⬤ *Murano glass is sold all around the world*

Luigi Camozzo Specialist in fine, engraved glass. ⓐ Fondamenta Venier 3 ① 041 736 875 ② 11.00–13.30, 14.30–18.00 Mon–Fri, closed Sat & Sun ⓝ Water bus to Venier

Marina e Susanna Sent Contemporary designer glass jewellery. ⓐ Fondamenta Serenella 20 ① 041 527 4665 ⓦ www.marina esusannasent.com ② 10.00–18.00 Mon–Sat, closed Sun ⓝ Water bus to Colonna

Rossana e Rossana Traditional Venetian glass, but with modern variations as well. ⓐ Riva Lunga 11 ⓣ 041 527 4076 ⓛ 10.00–18.00 daily ⓦ Water bus to Museo

Venini Old and new designs in this well-established glass-making outlet. ⓐ Fondamenta dei Vetrai 50 ⓣ 041 273 7211 ⓦ www.venini. com ⓛ 09.30–17.30 Mon–Sat, closed Sun ⓦ Water bus to Colonna

BURANO

Emilia Arguably the best lace shop on Burano. ⓐ Piazza Galuppi 205 ⓣ 041 735 299 ⓦ www.emiliaburano.it ⓛ 09.30–18.00 daily ⓦ Water bus to Burano

Martina Wide range of lace items including clothing. ⓐ Via San Mauro 307 ⓣ 041 735 523 ⓦ www.martina-lace.com ⓛ 09.30–18.00 daily ⓦ Water bus to Burano

BURANO LACE

The intricate craft of lacemaking was done by the wives of local fishermen from the 15th century. It almost died out but was happily revived in the 19th century. Visit the **Museo del Merletto** (Lace Museum). Set up in 1871 as a lacemaking school, it now displays some superb examples of Burano's famously intricate work, some dating from the 16th century. You can also occasionally see lacemakers at work. ⓐ Piazza Galuppi 187 ⓣ 041 730 034 ⓦ www.museicivicivenezia ni.it ⓛ 10.00–18.00 Wed–Mon, closed Tues (Apr–Oct); 10.00–17.00 Wed–Mon, closed Tues (Nov–Mar); last entry 15 mins before closing ⓦ Water bus to Burano ⓘ Admission charge

TAKING A BREAK & AFTER DARK

Al Gatto Nero ££ ❶ A friendly place with excellent fresh fish.
📍 Fondamenta della Giudecca 88, Burano 📞 041 730 120 🕐 12.00–
15.00, 18.00–22.00 Tues–Sun, closed Mon 🚤 Water bus to Burano

Al Trono di Attila ££ ❷ Traditional Venetian food served in a pretty
garden. 📍 Fondamenta Borgognoni 7A, Torcello 📞 041 730 094 🕐 Lunch
& dinner 🚤 Water bus to Museo ℹ Min 8 people, booking essential

Alla Maddalena ££ ❸ This lunchtime restaurant on a little island near
Burano serves game in winter and fish during summer. 📍 Mazzorbo
📞 041 730 151 🕐 12.00–15.00 Fri–Wed, dinner Fri–Wed, closed Thur
🚤 Water bus to Mazzorbo ℹ Min 8 people, booking essential

Da Romano ££ ❹ Traditional lagoon fish and seafood dishes. 📍 Piazza
Galuppi 221, Burano 📞 041 730 030 🕐 12.00–15.00, 18.30–20.00 Mon
& Wed–Sat, 12.00–15.00 Sun, closed Tues 🚤 Water bus to Burano

ACCOMMODATION

Locanda Cipriani ££–£££ Run by a branch of the Cipriani family since
the 1930s, this restaurant and small hotel is one of the best-known
places in the lagoon. The simple, elegant restaurant spills out on to
a charming terrace and garden and is a good place to enjoy an
afternoon drink. 📍 Piazza Santa Fosca 29, Torcello 📞 041 730 150
🕐 12.00–15.00 Wed, Thur, Sun & Mon, 12.00–15.00, 19.15–21.00 Fri &
Sat, closed Tues 🌐 www.locandacipriani.com 🚤 Water bus to Torcello

---

▶ *All sorts of water transport travel up and down the waterways of Venice*

PRACTICAL
information

Directory

GETTING THERE

By air

Venice's main airport **Marco Polo** (see page 48) has regular direct flights from the UK with British Airways (ⓦ www.ba.com), Lufthansa (ⓦ www.lufthansa.com), bmi baby (ⓦ www.bmibaby.com) and easyJet (ⓦ www.easyjet.com). Alitalia (ⓦ www.alitalia.com) offers flights via Milan. Ryanair (ⓦ www.ryanair.com) flies to **Treviso** (see page 50) airport, around 40 km (25 miles) from Venice.

There are direct flights to Venice from the US with Delta (ⓦ www.delta.com) and US Airways (ⓦ www.usairways.com).

An alternative route is to fly to Milan's **Malpensa** airport (ⓦ www.sea-aeroportimilano.it) and transfer to Venice by direct shuttle or train (ⓦ www.trenitalia.com).

Many people are aware that air travel emits CO_2, which contributes to climate change. You may be interested in the possibility of lessening the environmental impact of your flight through the charity **Climate Care** (ⓦ www.jpmorganclimatecare.com), which offsets your CO_2 by funding environmental projects around the world.

> ### RAIL TRAVEL IN STYLE
> A luxurious alternative to conventional rail travel is the Orient Express, which offers 28 trips from London to Venice between April and November. The journey takes 31 hours in the luxurious Venice Simplon-Orient Express train, with all meals included in the price. ☎ 0845 077 2222 ⓦ www.orient-express.com

By car

Venice is linked to the rest of Italy by major motorways. Travelling to Venice by car, however, is not recommended. You cannot drive anywhere in the city beyond Piazzale Roma and parking is both expensive and limited. See page 50 for advice on parking.

By coach

Coach travel is one of the cheapest but slowest ways to reach Venice from the UK. The journey takes 25–30 hours from London Victoria coach station. Contact **Eurolines** ☎ 08705 143 219 ⓦ www.eurolines.com

By rail

The journey by train from London St Pancras International to Venice takes just over 17 hours, changing in Paris. If you fly to Milan and want to take the train to Venice from there, the rail journey takes around three hours.

For further information on rail travel within Italy see **Trenitalia** ⓦ www.trenitalia.com

Rail Europe offers information on train travel in Europe, including reservations and tickets. ⓦ www.raileurope.co.uk

The monthly *Thomas Cook European Rail Timetable* gives up-to-date schedules for European international and national train services. ☎ 01733 416 477 (UK); 1 800 322 3834 (USA) ⓦ www.thomascookpublishing.com

ENTRY FORMALITIES

EU citizens can remain in Italy for an unlimited period but should register with the city council after 90 days. Visitors from the US, Canada, Australia and New Zealand do not need visas for stays of up to three months, but South African visitors do require a visa. Everyone must show a valid passport or identity card (EU citizens only) upon entry to Italy.

EU citizens do not have to declare goods imported or exported as long as they are for their personal use and they have arrived from another country within the EU. For non-EU citizens or arrivals from outside the EU, the following import restrictions apply: 400 cigarettes or 200 small cigars or 100 cigars or 500 g of tobacco; 1 litre of spirits or 2 litres of fortified wine; 50 g of perfume; €10,000 in cash. See ⓦ www.agenziadogane.it for more information on customs regulations.

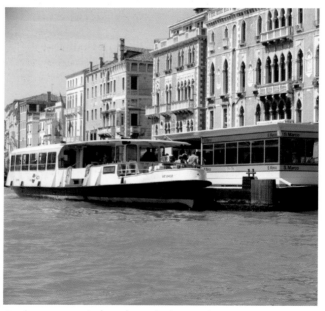

⬢ *Water buses are reliable and comfortable*

MONEY

Italy is a member of the European Union and the euro (€) is the official currency. There are seven banknotes: €5, €10, €20, €50, €100, €200 and €500. Coins come in denominations of €1, €2 and 1, 2, 5, 10, 20 and 50 cents.

There are 24-hour ATM machines located outside most banks, as well as at airports and railway stations, accepting Cirrus, Maestro, Visa and MasterCard.

Foreign currencies and traveller's cheques can be changed at most banks and bureaux de change with a passport or other ID, or at hotels for a hefty commission.

Visa and MasterCard credit cards are commonly accepted in larger stores and hotels but be aware that many bars, cafés, small shops and restaurants do not accept credit and debit cards. Make sure you have some cash in euros, particularly when you arrive.

HEALTH, SAFETY & CRIME

Tap water is safe to drink in Venice and hygiene standards in restaurants are high. Be careful of eating too much seafood if you are not used to it and take mosquito repellent in summer.

UK citizens are entitled to the same medical care as Italians on production of a European Health Insurance Card (EHIC Ⓦ www.ehic.org.uk). Your hotel or the tourist office should be able to advise you of local surgeries and doctors on call. You will have to pay upfront for your visit so don't forget to keep proof of payment in order to be reimbursed when you arrive home. Medicine and tests may cost extra and dentists are not covered by the EHIC. It is advisable to take out comprehensive travel insurance.

Non-EU nationals are entitled to free emergency medical care but should take out medical insurance for all other situations.

Pharmacies (*farmacie*) have green cross signs outside and staff are qualified to give advice about minor ailments. If you use a particular medication regularly, it is a good idea to take a stock with you.

Venice is generally safe for travellers, although as with any city you should avoid walking alone at night and in quiet streets. Pick-pocketing, unfortunately, is common in San Marco, the Rialto and other crowded areas including the railway station and water buses. Make sure you keep your wallet safely hidden, your bags zipped shut, and your camera firmly in your hand with the strap around your neck. Leave your passport and valuables in the hotel safe.

LOST PROPERTY

The main *ufficio oggetti smarriti* (lost property office) is at ⓐ San Marco 4136, Riva del Carbon ⓣ 041 274 8225 ⓛ 08.30–12.30 Mon–Fri, closed Sat & Sun. If you lose any belongings while using public transport, contact the ACTV office at Santa Croce or Piazzale Roma ⓣ 041 2722 1279 ⓛ 07.00–19.30 daily. The Santa Lucia railway station lost property office is on platform 14 ⓣ 041 785 531

OPENING HOURS

Most major attractions are open between 09.00 or 10.00 and 18.00, closing on Mondays. Winter opening hours are generally shorter, and smaller museums and churches may close for lunch.

Banks generally open 08.30–13.00 Mon–Fri, and sometimes 14.45–15.45. They are closed on public holidays and work shorter hours the day before.

Shops open 09.00 or 10.00 until 19.00 or 19.30 Mon–Sat, sometimes closing for lunch. Some shops close on Mondays. All-day and Sunday opening is common in tourist hotspots. Most

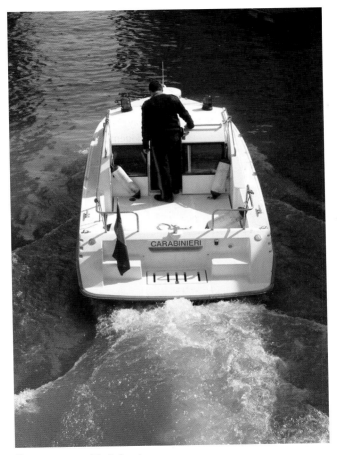

⬤ The police patrol Venice's waterways

supermarkets are open 09.00–19.30 Mon–Sat. Food markets are open from early in the morning until midday. The Rialto tourist market is open all day but the food market closes at noon.

Pharmacies are usually open 09.00–13.00, 16.00–20.00 Mon–Sat. Details of out-of-hours pharmacies are posted on a sign on the door.

The opening hours of bars, cafés and restaurants vary greatly, but very few in Venice are open past midnight. Hot meals are generally only served at specific times – around 12.00–14.30 for lunch and 19.00–22.00 for dinner – but snacks may be served throughout the day.

ⓘ Many establishments, particularly restaurants, close for two weeks in winter and again in July or August.

TOILETS

Public toilets in Venice are relatively well signposted and are normally open 08.00–20.00. Be prepared to pay a small fee, usually €0.50. There are two public toilets near St Mark's Square (one at the Giardinetti Reali) and others at the Rialto, the railway station, Piazzale Roma, in front of the Accademia Gallery and in the districts of Cannaregio and Castello.

Museums sometimes have clean toilets in the publicly accessible areas near the entrance. Hotels are also a good bet. If you want to use the toilet in a bar or café, it is polite to have a quick drink there also.

CHILDREN

Children are welcome in most restaurants and cafés, particularly the simpler ones, and there are plenty of ice cream and cake shops to keep them fed and happy. Public places, including restaurants and bars, are now smoke-free by law.

Baby food, nappies and other children's essentials are best bought from supermarkets, and some pharmacies may also stock what you need. Supermarkets tend to be fairly hard to find in the city centre so try to bring adequate supplies with you from home, along with any medication. Try the **Coop** (ⓐ Santa Croce 506A, Piazzale Roma ⓛ 08.30–20.00 daily) or **Billa** (ⓐ Dorsoduro 1491, Zattere ⓛ 08.30–20.00 daily).

Your children may not be thrilled at the idea of traipsing round museums and churches but they'll love the views from the top of the **Campanile** in St Mark's Square (see page 65) and the scale models at the excellent **Naval History Museum** (see page 72). The **Peggy Guggenheim Collection** (see page 86) offers children's workshops on Sundays and some civic museums also organise family days (see ⓦ www.museiciviciveneziani.it). The dungeons at the **Doge's Palace** (see page 66) are always popular.

Sometimes the simplest activities are the best – just crossing the canal on a gondola, taking a ride on the water bus or splashing out on a spin in a water taxi can be a great way to keep children entertained. If you are confident handling a boat, hire a small one from **Cristiano Brussa** (ⓐ Cannaregio 1030, Fondamenta di Cannaregio ⓣ 041 275 0196 ⓦ www.cristianobrussa.com).

Green spaces in Venice aren't huge, but **Campo Santo Stefano** (see page 69), Campo San Polo (see page 94) and the **Giardini Pubblici** in Castello (see page 60) are fine for a lazy afternoon playing around. If you visit during the **Biennale festival** (see page 9), you can spend long, happy afternoons visiting the exhibitions in the Arsenale and Giardini sites. Or go to Parco Savorgnan in Cannaregio to beat a leafy retreat.

For a change of scenery, take children to watch the glass-blowing demonstrations on the island of Murano (see page 135), or the lacemaking on Burano (see page 137). And for most children, you can't go wrong if you buy a bucket and spade and head to the Lido for some beach-side fun (see page 120).

COMMUNICATIONS

Internet

Internet cafés, Wi-Fi and hotels providing Internet access are increasingly available in Venice, with many bars increasingly offering free Internet access if you buy a drink. Photo ID is required at Internet cafés.

Venice is now a Wi-Fi city. To find out about how to connect and for the various options, go to Ⓦ www.veniceconnected.com.

Internet Corner ❷ Castello 6661A, Barbaria delle Tole ❶ 041 277 0515 🕒 10.00–22.00 Mon–Sat, closed Sun

Venetian Navigator Two centrally located Internet cafés. ❸ San Marco 5239, Calle degli Stagneri ❶ 041 522 8649 and ❸ San Marco 5300, Calle Casselleria ❶ 041 227 1056 🕒 10.00–20.30 daily (Apr–Sept); 10.00–19.30 daily (Oct–Mar)

Phone

Phone boxes take *schede telefoniche* (phonecards), which can be bought at newsstands or *tabacchi* (tobacconists). Calling rates from phone boxes and hotels tend to be very high. If you travel to Italy often, it may be worth purchasing an Italian SIM card for your mobile.

Telephoning Venice

The area code for the whole of Venice, including the Lido and lagoon islands, is 041. Telephone numbers beginning 800 are toll-free, and

TELEPHONING ABROAD

From Italy, dial 00, followed by your country code (UK 44; Republic of Ireland 353; US and Canada 1; Australia 61; New Zealand 64; South Africa 27), followed by the area code (leaving out the first 'o' if there is one) and then the local number you require.

numbers beginning 03 are mobile phones. The international dialling code for Italy is 39. To call Venice from abroad, dial either 00 (from the UK), 011 (from the US) or 0011 (from Australia), followed by the international code (39), followed by the area code (041) and then the local number you require. Note that, unlike in many countries, when telephoning Italy from abroad you do not drop the initial 'o' of the area code.

Post

Postal services in Italy are generally reliable. It is worth paying a little extra for *poste priorità* (express post), which needs a special *priorità* sticker, as this will ensure your letters arrive quickly. Postboxes are red and affixed to building walls. They have two slots – one for letters to be delivered within Venice (*per la Città*) and one for all other destinations and abroad (*Altre Destinazioni*). Stamps can be bought in tobacconists as well as in post offices (*ufficio postale*).

Central post office ⓐ San Marco 5016, Mercceria ⓑ 08.30–18.30 Mon–Fri, 08.30–13.30 Sat, closed Sun

ELECTRICITY

Electrical current in Italy is 220V AC and plugs are the standard European two round-pin ones. British appliances will need a simple adaptor; these are available in airports and hardware shops but are best obtained in the UK before travelling. US and other equipment designed for 110V will usually need a transformer (*transformatore di corrente*) in addition to an adaptor.

TRAVELLERS WITH DISABILITIES

Venice is an old city and not naturally suited to travellers with physical disabilities. The canals, steep bridges and narrow bumpy streets can be a challenge, particularly when it is crowded. Access facilities are improving rapidly, however, with ramps over bridges and lifts in museums being installed. Importantly, all ACTV water buses are step-free and fairly easy to negotiate for travellers in wheelchairs. Gondolas require several steps and some agility to board.

Be aware that not all hotels and restaurants advertising disabled access actually have accessible facilities such as disabled toilets. Many hotels and museums do not have lifts. It is best to check beforehand and be clear about your needs.

Private beaches on the Lido have disabled toilets, which you can use if you hire a beach hut or umbrella for the day. There are also public disabled toilets on the Lido as well as on the islands of Torcello, Burano and Murano.

Thankfully, there is a good source of up-to-date information on accessibility available from the Informhandicap service at the city council's Ufficio Relazioni con il Pubblico (public relations office), including specific brochures, guides and maps of the city indicating the location of disabled toilets and bridges with wheelchair ramps. ❸ Ca' Farsetti, San Marco 4136 ❶ 041 274 8945 Ⓦ www.comune.venezia.it/handicap ❷ informahandicap@comune.venezia.it Ⓛ 09.00–13.00 Thur, closed Fri–Wed

RADAR is the main source of information for UK-based travellers.
ⓐ 12 City Forum, 250 City Rd, London EC1V 8AF ⓣ 020 7250 3222
ⓦ www.radar.org.uk
SATH (Society for Accessible Travel & Hospitality) advises US-based
travellers with disabilities. ⓐ 347 Fifth Ave, Suite 610, New York,
NY 10016 ⓣ 212 447 7284 ⓦ www.sath.org

TOURIST INFORMATION

Venice's local tourist information office is APT (Azienda Promozione
Turistica di Venezia). It is an excellent source of information,
supplying maps, events listings and guidebooks. It does not offer
an accommodation booking service but can provide lists and advice.
See also its helpful website ⓦ www.turismovenezia.it. Offices are
open all year round except at Christmas and New Year.

USEFUL WEBSITES

Water bus, road bus and ferry services: ⓦ www.actv.it
The city council: ⓦ www.comune.venezia.it
The main churches: ⓦ www.chorusvenezia.org
Civic museums: ⓦ www.museiciviciveneziani.it
Maps and events listings: ⓦ www.ombra.net and
www.veniceonline.it
Transport and events: ⓦ www.hellovenezia.com
Carnival: ⓦ www.carnivalofvenice.com
The online version of the excellent listings magazine
Un Ospite di Venezia (A Guest in Venice):
ⓦ www.unospitedivenezia.it. Printed copies are available
from tourist offices and hotels.

Lido ⓐ Gran Viale Maria Elisabetta 6A ⓣ 041 529 8711 ⓛ 09.00–12.30, 15.30–18.00 daily (June–Oct); closed Nov–May

Marco Polo airport ⓣ 041 541 5887 ⓛ 09.30–19.30 daily

Piazzale Roma ⓐ ASM Garage (located within the garage) ⓣ 041 241 1499 ⓛ 09.30–13.00, 13.30–16.30 daily

San Marco ⓐ Piazza San Marco 71F ⓣ 041 529 8711 ⓛ 09.00–15.30 daily

San Marco ⓐ Giardinetti Reali 2 ⓣ 041 529 8711 ⓛ 10.00–18.00 daily

Santa Lucia railway station ⓣ 041 529 8711 ⓛ 08.00–18.30 daily

⬤ *Buildings with beautiful Venetian windows line the canals*

BACKGROUND READING

Don't Look Now by Daphne Du Maurier. Du Maurier's short story was made into a controversial Anglo-Italian thriller film in 1973.

Painting in Renaissance Venice by Peter Humfrey. A comprehensive account of the painting in Venice during this period.

The Architecture of Venice by Deborah Howard. The definitive guide to the architecture of the city.

The Merchant of Venice by William Shakespeare.

Venice: A Maritime Republic by Frederick C Lane. A succinct account of the history of Venice as a major sea power.

Emergencies

The following are free-pay emergency numbers:
Ambulance ☎ 118
Coastguard ☎ 1530
Fire ☎ 115
Police ☎ 112

MEDICAL SERVICES

Ospedale Civile is Venice's main hospital with a 24-hour *Pronto Soccorso* (Accident & Emergency) department ⓐ Castello 6777, Campo Santi Giovanni e Paolo ☎ 041 529 4111

Ospedale al Mare is the Lido's hospital ⓐ Lungomare D'Annunzio 1, Lido ☎ 041 526 1544

POLICE

There are three types of police in Venice: the paramilitary *carabinieri*, the *polizia* (state police) and the *vigili* (local police). All will help in an emergency and there are plenty patrolling tourist areas.

If you are the victim of a crime, go straight to a *questura* (police station) to make a report. You will need the paperwork to claim on your insurance. There are police stations at:

ⓐ Castello 4693A, Campo San Zaccaria ☎ 041 520 4777
Ⓝ Water bus: San Zaccaria
ⓐ Castello 5053, Fondamenta di San Lorenzo ☎ 041 270 5511
Ⓝ Water bus: San Zaccaria
ⓐ Santa Croce 500, Piazzale Roma ☎ 041 271 5511 Ⓝ Water bus: Piazzale Roma
ⓐ Via Dardanelli 52, Lido ☎ 041 220 7911
State police Ⓦ http://questure.poliziadistato.it/Venezia

EMBASSIES & CONSULATES

Australian Embassy ⓐ Via Antonio Bosio 5, Rome ⓣ 06 852 721
ⓦ www.italy.embassy.gov.au

British Consulate ⓐ Piazza Donatori di Sangue 2, Mestre ⓣ 041 505 5990

British Embassy ⓐ Via XX Settembre 80, Rome ⓣ 06 4220 0001
ⓦ http://ukinitaly.fco.gov.uk

Canadian Embassy ⓐ Via Zara 30, Rome ⓣ 06 854 442 911 (consular section) ⓦ www.canada.it

Irish Embassy ⓐ Piazza di Campitelli 3, Rome ⓣ 06 697 9121
ⓦ www.ambasciata-irlanda.it

New Zealand Embassy ⓐ Via Clitunno 44, Rome ⓣ 06 853 7501
ⓦ www.nzembassy.com

South African Embassy ⓐ Via Tanaro 14, Rome ⓣ 06 852 541
ⓦ www.sudafrica.it

US Embassy ⓐ Via Vittorio Veneto 121, Rome ⓣ 06 46741
ⓦ http://italy.usembassy.gov

USEFUL PHRASES

Help!	**Fire!**	**Stop!**
Aiuto!	Al fuoco!	Ferma!
Ahyootaw!	*Ahl fooawcaw!*	*Fairmah!*

Call an ambulance/a doctor/the police/the fire service!
Chiamate un'ambulanza/un medico/la polizia/i pompieri!
Kyahmahteh oon ahmboolahntsa/oon mehdeecaw/lah pawleetsya/ee pompee-ehree!

ACKNOWLEDGEMENTS

Thomas Cook Publishing wishes to thank the photographers, picture libraries and other organisations, to whom the copyright belongs, for the photographs in this book.

Francesco Allegretto, pages 5, 7, 14, 19, 23, 28, 36, 39, 43, 47, 59, 77, 93, 101, 119 and 125; Bill Casey/BigStockPhoto.com, page 82; Paul Gardner/iStockphoto.com, page 104; Roland Nagy/SXC.hu, page 13; Margarit Ralev/SXC.hu, page 139; Bruno Schievano/SXC.hu, pages 152–3; Anwer Bati, all others.

Project editor: Rosalind Munro
Layout: Paul Queripel
Proofreaders: Karolin Thomas & Cath Senker

Send your thoughts to
books@thomascook.com

- **Found a great bar, club, shop or must-see sight that we don't feature?**

- **Like to tip us off about any information that needs a little updating?**

- **Want to tell us what you love about this handy little guidebook and more importantly how we can make it even handier?**

Then here's your chance to tell all! Send us ideas, discoveries and recommendations today and then look out for your valuable input in the next edition of this title.

Email the above address (stating the title) or write to: pocket guides Series Editor, Thomas Cook Publishing, PO Box 227, Coningsby Road, Peterborough PE3 8SB, UK.

WHAT'S IN YOUR GUIDEBOOK?

Independent authors Impartial up-to-date information from our travel experts who meticulously source local knowledge.

Experience Thomas Cook's 165 years in the travel industry and guidebook publishing enriches every word with expertise you can trust.

Travel know-how Thomas Cook has thousands of staff working around the globe, all living and breathing travel.

Editors Travel-publishing professionals, pulling everything together to craft a perfect blend of words, pictures, maps and design.

You, the traveller We deliver a practical, no-nonsense approach to information, geared to how you really use it.

Useful phrases

English	Italian	Approx pronunciation
BASICS		
Yes	Sì	See
No	No	Noh
Please	Per favore	Pehr fahvohreh
Thank you	Grazie	Grahtsyeh
Hello	Buongiorno/Ciao	Bwonjohrnoh/Chow
Goodbye	Arrivederci/Ciao	Ahreevehderchee/Chow
Excuse me	Scusi	Skoozee
Sorry	Mi dispiace	Mee deespyahcheh
That's okay	Va bene	Vah behneh
I don't speak Italian	Non parlo italiano	Non pahrloh eetahlyahnoh
Do you speak English?	Parla inglese?	Pahrlah eenglehzeh?
Good morning	Buongiorno	Bwonjohrnoh
Good afternoon	Buon pomeriggio	Bwon pohmehreejoh
Good evening	Buona sera	Bwonah sehrah
Goodnight	Buona notte	Bwonah nohteh
My name is ...	Mi chiamo ...	Mee kyahmoh ...
NUMBERS		
One	Uno	Oonoh
Two	Due	Dooeh
Three	Tre	Treh
Four	Quattro	Kwahttroh
Five	Cinque	Cheenkweh
Six	Sei	Say
Seven	Sette	Sehteh
Eight	Otto	Ohtoh
Nine	Nove	Nohveh
Ten	Dieci	Dyehchee
Twenty	Venti	Ventee
Fifty	Cinquanta	Cheenkwahntah
One hundred	Cento	Chentoh
SIGNS & NOTICES		
Airport	Aeroporto	Ahehrohpohrtoh
Railway station	Stazione ferroviaria	Statsyoneh fehrohveeahreeyah
Platform	Binario	Beenahreeyoh
Smoking/non-smoking	Fumatori/non fumatori	Foomahtohree/non foomahtohree
Toilets	Bagni	Bahnyee
Ladies/Gentlemen	Signore/Signori	Seenyoreh/Seenyohree
Subway	Metropolitana	Mehtrohpohleetahnah